Functional Skills

Maths

Entry Level 3

This book is for anyone doing Entry Level 3 Functional Skills Maths.
It covers everything you need, whichever exam board you're studying.

All the topics are explained in a straightforward way, with test-style
questions to give you plenty of realistic practice before the final test.

Since 1995, CGP study books have helped millions of students do well
in their tests and exams. We cover dozens of subjects for all ages
— and we always keep our prices as low as possible.

Study & Test Practice

Contents

Section One — Number

Numbers 1
Adding and Subtracting 5
Multiplying and Dividing 9
Decimals 13
More on Decimals 16
Fractions 18
Rounding 22
Estimating 24
Number Patterns 26

Section Two — Measure

Units 28
Length 31
Perimeter 35
Weight 37
Capacity 40
Temperature 44
Scales 47
Money 50

Section Three — Dates and Time

Calendars 54
Time 56
Timetables 60

Section Four — Shape and Space

Angles..63

Lines of Symmetry...64

2D Shapes...66

3D Shapes...69

Plans..71

Movement and Direction..73

Section Five — Handling Data

Lists...75

Tables..77

Charts and Graphs...80

Test-style Questions

Test Help...84

Task 1 — An Evening Out..85

Task 2 — Hosting a Dinner Party...88

Task 3 — Buying a Car..91

Task 4 — Going on Holiday...94

Task 5 — A Car Boot Sale...98

Answers — Practice Questions..101

Answers — Test-style Questions...104

Glossary..106

Index..108

Published by CGP

Editors:
Katie Braid, Jane Ellingham, Christopher Lindle, Hayley Thompson.

Contributor:
George MacDonald.

With thanks to Katherine Craig, Anna Gainey, David Norden,
Glenn Rogers and Karen Wells for the proofreading.

ISBN: 978 1 84762 873 2

Groovy website: www.cgpbooks.co.uk

Printed by Elanders Ltd, Newcastle upon Tyne.
Jolly bits of clipart from CorelDRAW®

Photocopying – it's dull, grey and sometimes a bit naughty. Luckily, it's dead cheap, easy and quick to order more copies of this book from CGP – just call us on 0870 750 1242. Phew!
Text, design, layout and original illustrations © Coordination Group Publications Ltd. (CGP) 2013
All rights reserved.

Section One — Number

Numbers

All Numbers are Made of Digits

1) A digit is just one of these:

   0   1   2   3   4   5   6   7   8   9

2) All numbers are made by putting these digits together.

3) For example, 21, 48, 321 or 648.

Two-digit Numbers

The first digit of a two-digit number tells you how many tens the number has.

The second digit tells you how many units (ones) the number has.

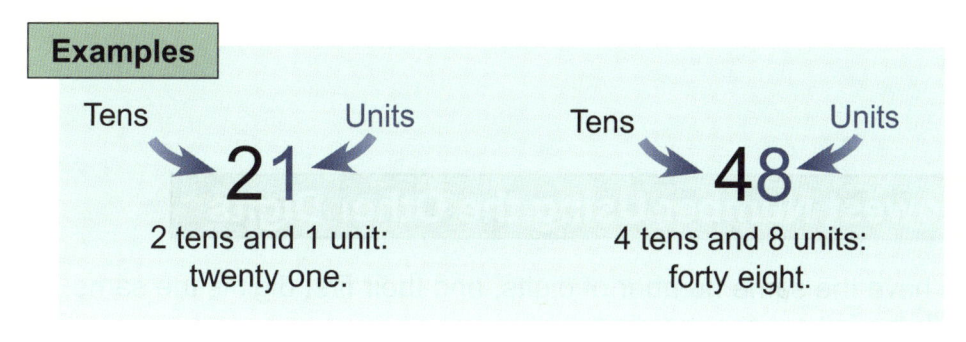

Examples

Tens → 2**1** ← Units

2 tens and 1 unit: twenty one.

Tens → 4**8** ← Units

4 tens and 8 units: forty eight.

Three-digit Numbers

The first digit of a three-digit number tells you how many hundreds the number has.

The second digit tells you how many tens the number has.

The third digit tells you how many units the number has.

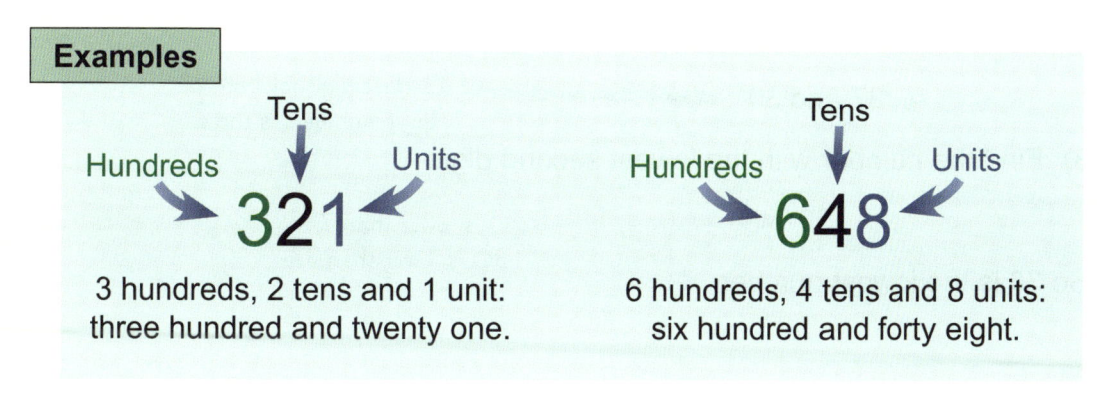

Examples

Hundreds → **3**2**1** ← Units (Tens ↓)

3 hundreds, 2 tens and 1 unit: three hundred and twenty one.

Hundreds → **6**4**8** ← Units (Tens ↓)

6 hundreds, 4 tens and 8 units: six hundred and forty eight.

Finding the Lowest Number From the First Digit

1) First find the numbers with the fewest digits.

2) From these, find the one with the lowest first digit. That's the lowest number.

> **Example**
>
> Fernando has £345, Sunita has £3, Jane has £8, Chris has £341.
> Who has the least money?
>
> *Least, smallest and fewest just mean lowest.*
>
> 1) Find the numbers with the fewest digits:
>
>   £3 and £8 ← These both have just one digit.
>
> 2) Find the number with the lowest first digit:
>
>   £3 ← 3 is lower than 8.
>
> So **Sunita** has the least money.

Finding the Lowest Number Using the Other Digits

1) If two numbers have the same number of digits, and their first digit is the same, find the one with the lowest second digit.

2) If the second digit is also the same, find the one with the lowest third digit.

> **Example**
>
> Find the lowest number from this list:
>
> 183, 37, 210, 30, 410, 52
>
> 1) Find the numbers with the fewest digits:
>
>   37, 30 and 52 ← These all have two digits.
>
> 2) Find the number with the lowest first digit:
>
>   37 and 30 ← The first digit for both of these numbers is three.
>
> 3) Find the number with the lowest second digit:
>
>   30 ← 0 is lower than 7, so 30 is lower than 37.
>
> So **30** is the lowest number.

Section One — Number

Finding the Highest Number Using the First Digit

1) First find the numbers with the most digits.

2) From these, find the one with the highest first digit. That's the highest number.

> **Example**
>
> Find the highest number from this list:
>
> 183, 37, 210, 30, 410, 52
>
> 1) Find the numbers with the most digits:
>
> 183, 210, 410 ← These all have three digits.
>
> 2) Find the number with the highest first digit:
>
> 410 ← The first digit of 410 is 4, which is higher than 1 (in 183) and 2 (in 210).
>
> So **410** is the highest number.

Finding the Highest Number Using the Other Digits

1) If two numbers have the same number of digits and their first digit is the same, find the one with the highest second digit.

2) If the second digit is also the same, find the one with the highest third digit.

> **Example**
>
> Fernando has £345, Sunita has £3, Jane has £8, Chris has £341.
> Who has the most money?
>
> 1) Find the numbers with the most digits:
>
> £345, £341.
>
> *Biggest, most, greatest and largest just mean highest.*
>
> 2) Find the number with the highest first digit:
>
> They're both 3.
>
> 3) Find the number with the highest second digit:
>
> They're both 4
>
> 4) Find the number with the highest third digit:
>
> £345 ← The third digit of 345 is 5, which is higher than the third digit of 341 (which is 1).
>
> So **Fernando** has the most money.

Practice Questions

1) Find the smallest number in this list:
   190, 27, 5, 16, 3, 210

   ....

2) Find the highest number in this list:
   190, 27, 5, 16, 3, 210

   ....

3) Phil has 6 days of holiday left, Colm has 14, Dorothy has 17 and Jill has 2.
   Who has the most days of holiday left?

   ....

4) The table below shows how much money four people have in their bank accounts.

Sarah	£424
Heather	£473
Katie	£452
Jane	£475

   a) Who has the most money in their account?

      ....

   b) Who has the least money in their account?

      ....

5) A flat pack wardrobe comes with the following screws:
   10 small gold, 15 large gold, 4 small silver and 25 large silver.

   a) What type of screw is the most common?

      ....

   b) Which screw is there the fewest of?

      ....

Section One — Number

Adding and Subtracting

You Need to Know When to Add

1) The questions you get in the test will be based on real-life situations.
2) You won't always be told what calculation to do to answer the question.
3) You'll need to work out for yourself what calculation to do.
4) Sometimes it will involve adding numbers together.
5) Addition is shown by a + sign.

Example 1

Charlene is ordering some tickets online.
The costs of the tickets, booking fee and delivery are shown below.

How much will one ticket cost her in total if she picks it up herself?

Ticket	£12
Booking fee	£2
Delivery	£3

Answer: you need to add together the price of a ticket plus the booking fee. You don't need to add on the delivery fee because Charlene is picking up the ticket herself. So the calculation you need to do is:

$$12 + 2 = £14$$

Sometimes you need to include units in your answer. Units tell you what type of number you've got. In this case the units are pounds, '£'.

Example 2

Janice is cleaning her house. How long it takes to clean each room is shown below. How long does it take to clean all the rooms?

| Kitchen, 2 hours | Dining room, 1 hour |
| Living room, 2 hours | Bathroom, 1 hour |

Answer: you need to add together the times for all the rooms.
So the calculation you need to do is:

$$2 + 1 + 2 + 1 = 6 \text{ hours}$$ ← The units here are 'hours'.

Section One — Number

You Need to Know When to Subtract

1) Sometimes you'll need to subtract — take one number away from another.

2) Subtraction is shown using a – sign.

Example 1

Warren is paying for some crisps. The crisps cost £2.
He pays with a £10 note. How much change should he get back?

Answer: you need to take away how much the crisps cost from how much money he paid with. So the calculation you need to do is:

10 – 2 = £8

Example 2

Sybil works a 7 hour shift.

Her notes for her time sheet are shown on the right.

How long did she spend packing?

Picking	2 hours
Phones	4 hours
Packing	?

Answer: you need to take away the times you know from the total time she is at work. So the calculation you need to do is:

7 – 2 – 4 = 1 hour is spent packing.

Sometimes there is more than one way to answer a question. For example, here you could have added together the two times you knew (2 + 4 = 6) and then taken that away from 7 (7 – 6 = 1). As long as your method and answer are correct, you'll get the marks.

You Might Need to Add and Subtract

Example

Suri orders salmon and then lemon tart. She has a voucher for £2 off any meal. How much does she have to pay for lunch?

Answer: this calculation has two steps.

1) Add up the price of the meal: 10 + 4 = 14

2) Then take away the voucher: 14 – 2 = 12

Suri has to pay £12.

Salmon	£10
Roast Chicken	£10
Lemon Tart	£4
Cheesecake	£3

Section One — Number

Always Check Your Answer

1) Adding and subtracting are opposite calculations.

2) Once you've got your answer, you can check it using the opposite calculation.

3) You should get back to the number you started with.

Example 1

What is 176 − 12?

Answer: 176 − 12 = 164

You can use a calculator to work this out. You'll be able to take a calculator into the test and use it whenever you need to. There's a bit more on calculators below.

Check it using the opposite calculation: 164 + 12 = 176

Example 2

What is 9 + 15?

Answer: 9 + 15 = 24

You only need to do one of these calculations to check your answer.

Check it using the opposite calculation: 24 − 9 = 15   OR   24 − 15 = 9

Using a Calculator

1) Make sure it says '0' before you start.

2) Press the buttons carefully.

3) Always check the display to make sure you've pressed the right button.

4) Press the [=] button at the end of every calculation.

5) You can add and subtract using a calculator.

Example

James wants to buy a new fridge. One fridge costs £155 and another costs £130. What is the difference in price between the two fridges?

The calculation you need to do is 155 − 130.

[1][5][5][−][1][3][0][=]   [25]

Don't just write down 25 though. You need to think about what the answer on your calculator means and add in any units.

The difference in price is **£25**.

Section One — Number

Practice Questions

1) What is 2 + 3?

   ....

2) What is 25 + 14?

   ....

3) What is 20 − 4?

   ....

4) What is 176 − 98?

   ....

5) Tristan is buying a Blu-ray player. Model A is £78 and model B is £95.
   How much more expensive is model B?

   ....

6) Crissy has 742 packs of Christmas cards. She sells 337.
   How many packs does she have left?

   ....

7) Amir has 75p in his pocket. He spends 60p but gets 2p back.
   How much money does Amir have now?

   ....

8) Geraint has 260 CDs. He sells 125 to one shop and 50 to another.
   He then buys another 35 from the wholesaler. How many CDs does Geraint have now?

   ....

   ....

9) Kristel has 49 notepads in her cupboard and 37 at her desk. How many notepads does
   Kristel have in total? Show how you check your answer.

   ....

   ....

Section One — Number

Multiplying and Dividing

You Need to Know When to Multiply

1) Some calculations will involve multiplication — one number "times" another.

2) Multiplication is shown using a × sign.

Example 1

Sharon needs to buy some flour for a cake. A packet of flour costs £2. Sharon needs 3 packets. How much does the flour cost Sharon in total?

£2 × 3 = £6

Example 2

Claude buys a bike.
He has to pay £126 a month for 4 months.
How much will Claude pay in total for the bike?

Answer: you need to calculate 126 times 4.

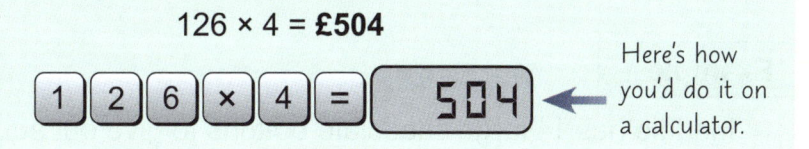

126 × 4 = **£504**

[1][2][6][×][4][=] 504 ← Here's how you'd do it on a calculator.

You Need to Know When to Divide

1) Some calculations will involve division.

2) Division is shown using a ÷ sign.

Example 1

Frank drives to work and back 5 days in a row.
He drives 50 miles in total.
How many miles does Frank drive each day?

Answer: the 50 miles needs to be divided by 5 days.
So you need to calculate 50 divided by 5.

50 ÷ 5 = **10 miles** ← The units here are 'miles'.

Section One — Number

> **Example 2**
>
> Lotte has gone out to dinner with 9 friends. The meal costs £280.
> The cost will be split equally between Lotte and her friends.
> How much will each person pay?
>
> Answer: Lotte is there with 9 friends,
> so that's 9 + 1 = 10 people in total.
> You need to calculate 280 divided by 10.
>
> 280 ÷ 10 = **£28**
>
> *Equally means everyone will pay the same amount.*
>
> 2 8 0 ÷ 1 0 = 28

Some Questions Need Answers that are Whole Numbers

1) You won't always end up with a whole number when you divide.

2) But sometimes, you'll need to give a whole number as your answer.

> **Example 1**
>
> Maddie has 14 large chocolate buttons to give out equally to her 5 students.
> How many buttons will each student get?
>
> Calculation: 14 ÷ 5 = 2.8
>
> You can't have 2.8 buttons, so the answer needs to be a whole number.
>
> 2.8 is between 2 and 3. There aren't enough buttons for 3 each.
> So Maddie will give each student **2 buttons**.

> **Example 2**
>
> Richard needs 75 chocolate biscuits for a coffee morning.
> The biscuits come in packs of 4. How many packs should Richard buy?
>
> Calculation: 75 ÷ 4 = 18.75
>
> Richard can't buy 18.75 packs, so your answer needs to be a whole number.
>
> 18.75 is between 18 and 19. If Richard buys 18 packs of biscuits,
> he won't have enough. So Richard will need to buy **19 packs**.

Practice Questions

1) What is 35 × 4?

   ....

2) What is 24 ÷ 2?

   ....

3) Cassandra has put out chairs for a concert. There are 25 rows of chairs.
   Each row has 5 chairs. How many chairs are there in total?

   ....

4) There are 14 screws in a packet. Justin buys 5 packets of screws. He needs 68 screws.
   Has Justin bought enough screws?

   ....

5) A secretary buys 3 boxes of A1 paper. Each box has 10 packets.
   There are 25 sheets of paper in each packet.

   a) How many sheets of paper are there in one box?

      ....

   b) How many sheets of paper has the secretary bought all together?

      ....

6) Connie needs to send 27 Christmas cards. The cards she likes come in packs of 5.
   How many packs should she buy?

   ....

   ....

7) Paula has 124 daffodils. She needs 10 daffodils to make a bunch.
   How many bunches of daffodils can she make?

   ....

   ....

Section One — Number

Always Check Your Answer

1) Multiplying and dividing are opposite calculations.

2) Once you've got your answer, you can check it using the opposite calculation.

3) You should get back to the number you started with.

> **Example 1**
>
> What is 137 × 4?
>
> Answer: 137 × 4 = 548
>
> Check it using the opposite calculation: 548 ÷ 4 = 137   OR   548 ÷ 137 = 4

> **Example 2**
>
> Stella needs 14 fabric heart patches to sew onto some bags.
> The hearts are sold in packs of 5. How many packs should Stella buy?
>
> Answer: 14 ÷ 5 = 2.8. Stella will need to buy 3 packs.
>
> Check it using the opposite calculation:
>
> 5 × 2 = 10 (not enough), 5 × 3 = 15 (enough). So Stella must buy 3 packs.

Practice Questions

1) What is 6 × 10? Show how you check your answer.

   ....

   ....

2) Rachael is pickling eggs. Each jar will hold 5 eggs. Rachael has 125 eggs in total.
   How many jars of pickled eggs can she make? Show how you check your answer.

   ....

   ....

3) Suzuki needs to send 18 invitations in the post. Stamps come in packs of 12.
   How many packs of stamps should Suzuki buy? Show how you check your answer.

   ....

   ....

Section One — Number

Decimals

Not All Numbers Are Whole Numbers

1) Decimals are numbers with a decimal point (.) in them. For example, 0.5, 1.3.

2) If you're saying the number out loud, you say "point" where the "." is.
   For example, 1.3 is one point three.

3) They're used to show the numbers in-between whole numbers.

4) Digits to the right of the "." are worth less than one.

> **Examples**
> - The number 0.9 is a bit smaller than the number 1.
> - The number 1.1 is a bit bigger than the number 1.
> - The number 1.9 is a bit smaller than the number 2.
> - The number 1.0 is the same as the number 1.
> - The number 1.5 is exactly halfway between the numbers 1 and 2.
> - The number 2.54 is bigger than the number 2.51.

You Can Show Decimals on a Number Line

1) A number line is a line with numbers spaced out along it in order.

2) The further right a number is on a number line, the bigger it is.

3) The space in-between the whole numbers can be split into divisions.

4) If the space is split into 10 divisions then each division is equal to 0.1.

5) You can see this on a number line:

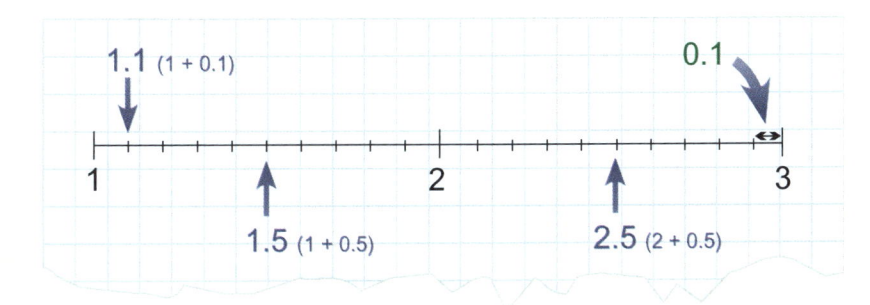

Section One — Number

Decimals are Used in Money and Measuring

1) Decimals are used in money to show pounds (£) and pence (p).

2) Money is always written with two digits after the decimal point, even if they're just 0s at the end.

Examples

- £7.38 means 7 pounds and 38 pence.
- You write £5.90 not £5.9 for 5 pounds and 90 pence.
- £5.09 is 5 pounds and 9 pence.

3) Decimals are also used in measuring.

4) For example, you can use them to show metres (m) and centimetres (cm).

Examples

- 3.20 m means 3 metres and 20 centimetres.
- 3.2 m means 3 m and 20 cm too. ← You don't need to have two digits after the point for measurements.
- 1.62 m means 1 m and 62 cm.

How to Put Decimals in Order

You might need to arrange a list of decimal numbers in order of size.

Example

Put these heights in order of size: 0.06 m, 2.1 m, 0.3 m.
Start with the largest.

1) Put the numbers into a column, lining up the decimal points.

2) Make all the numbers the same length by filling in extra zeros at the ends.

3) Look at the numbers before the decimal point. Arrange the numbers from largest to smallest.

4) If any of the numbers are the same, move on to the numbers after the decimal point. Arrange the numbers from largest to smallest.

Step 1:	Step 2:	Step 3:	Step 4:
0.06	0.06	2.10	2.10
2.1	2.10	0.06	0.30
0.3	0.30	0.30	0.06

The order is: 2.1 m, 0.3 m, 0.06 m.

Section One — Number

Finding the Largest or Smallest Decimal Number

You might need to give the largest or smallest number from a list of decimal numbers.

Example

Jan weighs 75.4 kg, Dylan weighs 52.5 kg and Andy weighs 75.9 kg.
Who weighs the most?

1) Find the number with the highest whole number:
   The numbers with the highest whole numbers are 75.4 kg and 75.9 kg.

2) Look at the first number after the decimal place.
   The one with the highest number is the largest:
   9 is bigger than 4, so 75.9 is the largest.

   You could also answer this by putting the numbers into size order, then reading off the largest one.

So **Andy** weighs the most.

Practice Questions

1) Is 11.32 smaller or bigger than 11.42?

   ....

2) Write 6 pounds and 43 pence as a decimal.

   ....

3) If Candice spends over £15 she gets free delivery. She spends £15.49. Is her delivery free?

   ....

4) Vehicles over 2.8 m tall can't go under a railway bridge. Joe's wagon is 2.84 m tall.
   Can he drive under the bridge?

   ....

5) Put these numbers in order starting with the smallest: 6.2, 7.9, 3.4, 7.8

   ....

6) Baz can lift 85.6 kg, Jess can lift 85.9 kg and Dan can lift 85.3 kg. Who is the strongest?

   ....

7) Flynn has £212.56, Aadi has £209.13 and Oliver has £212.59. Who has the most money?

   ....

Section One — Number

More on Decimals

Adding and Subtracting Decimals

1) You can add and subtract decimals using a calculator.
2) It's exactly the same as with whole numbers — just remember to type the decimal point into the calculator.

Example

Sooki wants to know how much she has spent shopping.

Potatoes £1.99

Cheese £2.99

Beans £0.59

Answer: add together everything Sooki has spent.

1.99 + 2.99 + 0.59 = £5.57

[1][.][9][9][+][2][.][9][9][+][0][.][5][9][=] 5.57

Multiplying and Dividing Decimals

You can multiply and divide decimals in exactly the same way as whole numbers.

Example

Ami is saving up for a new CD player.
She can afford to save £12.75 a month, for the next 10 months.
How much will she save in total in the next 10 months?

Answer: times the amount per month by the number of months.

12.75 × 10 = **£127.50**

[1][2][.][7][5][×][1][0][=] 127.5 ← Remember, money is always written with two numbers after the decimal point. So the answer is £127.50.

Section One — Number

Practice Questions

1) What is 1.99 + 2.99?

   ....

2) What is 15.99 − 10.50?

   ....

3) What is 3.5 × 5?

   ....

4) What is 7.8 ÷ 10?

   ....

5) Sonny wins £30 on a scratch card. He spends £6.15 of this in the shop.
   How much does he have left?

   ....

6) Nicola is buying a top for £24.99. She has a gift token for £12.50.
   How much does the top cost her?

   ....

7) Donald has a voucher for £2 off if he spends over £5 on fresh fruit.
   So far he has bought kiwis for £1.55 and strawberries for £2.85.
   Can he use his voucher?

   ....

8) Christie drives 13.2 miles each day. How many miles does she drive in 10 days?

   ....

9) Sanjay has 10.5 g of agar to share equally between two mixes.
   How much should he put into each mix?

   ....

10) Tim spends £36.75 on three books. Each book was the same price.
    How much did each book cost?

    ....

Section One — Number

Fractions

Fractions Show Parts of Things

1) If something is divided up into equal parts, you can show it as a fraction.

2) There are two bits to every fraction:

The bottom number shows how many parts there are in total. → $\frac{3}{7}$ ← The top number shows how many parts you're talking about.

Example

Colin has 4 pieces of cake. He eats 1 piece. What fraction did he eat?

He's eaten 1 out of the 4 pieces, so it's $\frac{1}{4}$ (you say 'one quarter').

How to Write Fractions

Here's how to write some common fractions:

One half = $\frac{1}{2}$ One third = $\frac{1}{3}$ One quarter = $\frac{1}{4}$ Three quarters = $\frac{3}{4}$

You can also get mixed fractions. Mixed fractions are when you have whole numbers and fractions together. For example, $1\frac{1}{4}$ (one and a quarter).

Practice Questions

1) Becca has 2 cans of pop. She drinks 1. What fraction did Becca drink?

    ....

2) Cliff had 4 desk calendars. He gave 3 away.

    a) How many calendars does he have left? ....

    b) What fraction of calendars does he have left?

    ....

Section One — Number

Fractions Show Divisions

1) $\frac{3}{4}$ is just another way of writing 3 ÷ 4.

2) So you can type fractions into your calculator by dividing the top by the bottom.

3) This turns them into decimals.

> **Example 1**
>
> What is $\frac{1}{2}$ as a decimal?
>
> $\frac{1}{2}$ is the same as 1 ÷ 2. So the calculation you need to do is: 1 ÷ 2 = **0.5**
>
> [1] [÷] [2] [=]   [0.5]

> **Example 2**
>
> What is $\frac{1}{4}$ + 2?
>
> $\frac{1}{4}$ is the same as 1 ÷ 4. So the calculation you need to do is: 1 ÷ 4 + 2 = **2.25**

'Of' means 'times'

1) Sometimes, you might need to calculate a 'fraction of' something.

2) In these cases, 'of' means 'times' (multiply).

> **Example 1**
>
> What is $\frac{3}{4}$ of £200?
>
> 1) 'Of' means 'times' (×), so $\frac{3}{4}$ of £200 is the same as $\frac{3}{4}$ × £200.
> 2) The overall calculation you need to do is: 3 ÷ 4 × 200 = **£150**
>
> [3] [÷] [4] [×] [2] [0] [0] [=]   [150]

Section One — Number

> **Example 2**
>
> To pass the test, Charlie must get $\frac{1}{2}$ of the answers correct. There are 130 answers in total. Charlie has got 67 correct. Has he passed the test?
>
> 1) $\frac{1}{2}$ of 130 is the same as $\frac{1}{2} \times 130$.
> 2) So the calculation you need to do is: $1 \div 2 \times 130 = 65$
>
> [1][÷][2][×][1][3][0][=]   65
>
> 3) 67 is greater than 65.
>
> So **yes**, Charlie passed the test.

Writing Fractions as Decimals

1) $\frac{1}{4}$ is the same as saying $1 \div 4 = 0.25$, which is a decimal.
2) Here's what some common fractions are written as decimals:

One half = $\frac{1}{2}$ = 0.5   One quarter = $\frac{1}{4}$ = 0.25   Three quarters = $\frac{3}{4}$ = 0.75

Ordering Fractions

1) Fractions are just numbers.
2) So they can be put in order of size like any other numbers.
3) From smallest to biggest: $\frac{1}{4} \to \frac{1}{3} \to \frac{1}{2} \to \frac{3}{4} \to 1$
4) Here it is on a number line:

$\frac{1}{4}$ = 0.25 $\frac{1}{2}$ = 0.5

0   1

$\frac{1}{3}$ = 0.33 $\frac{3}{4}$ = 0.75

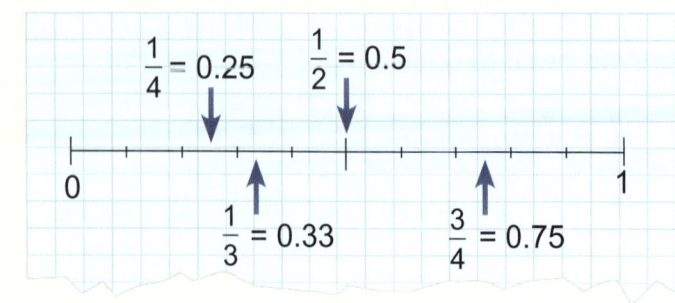

Section One — Number

> **Example**
>
> An office is buying some computers from either X-traComp Computers or Ultravision Computers. The computers cost the same price but X-traComp will give them $\frac{1}{2}$ off and Ultravision will give them $\frac{1}{3}$ off.
>
> Who should they buy the computers from? Give a reason for your answer.
>
> $\frac{1}{2}$ (0.5) is bigger than a $\frac{1}{3}$ (0.33).
>
> So they should buy them from X-traComp as they will be cheaper.

Practice Questions

1) What is $\frac{3}{4}$ written as a decimal?

   ....

2) What is $\frac{1}{3}$ of 9?

   ....

3) What is $\frac{1}{4}$ of 440?

   ....

4) What is $\frac{3}{4}$ of £250?

   ....

5) Felicity has £560 to spend on her two week holiday. She thinks she'll spend $\frac{1}{2}$ of the money each week. How much money will she spend each week?

   ....

6) Trisha is a manicurist. Her clients are late $\frac{1}{4}$ of the time. Trisha has 28 clients a week.

   a) How many are late each week?

   ....

   b) How many are on time each week?

   ....

Section One — Number

Rounding

Rounding to the Nearest 10

1) "Rounding to the nearest 10" means finding the nearest number ending in 0. For example, 10, 60, 230.

2) If the last digit is less than 5, round down to the ten below.

3) If the last digit is 5 or more, round up to the ten above.

> **Example**
>
> Sam has 32 sandwiches. How many does he have to the nearest 10?
>
> The last digit is 2. This is less than 5, so you need to round it down.
>
> Sam has **30 sandwiches** to the nearest 10.
>
> You can see this on a number line:
>
> Less than 5, so round down.
> 32 → 30 | 35 | 40

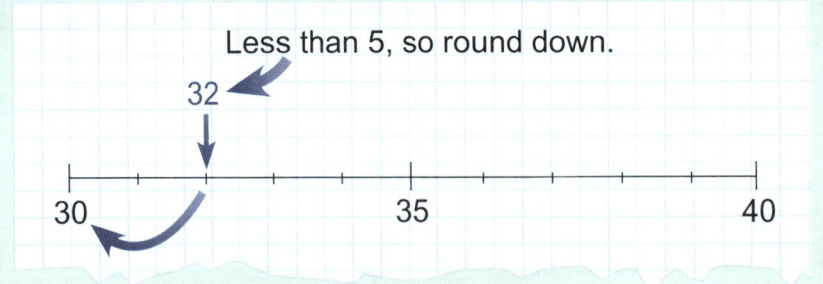

Rounding to the Nearest 100

1) "Rounding to the nearest 100" means finding the nearest number ending in 00. For example, 100, 600, 2300.

2) If the last two digits are less than 50, round down to the hundred below.

3) If the last two digits are more than 50, round up to the hundred above.

> **Example**
>
> Zara has 250 envelopes.
> How many envelopes does she have to the nearest hundred?
>
> The last two digits are 50, so round up to the hundred above.
>
> Zara has **300 envelopes** to the nearest hundred.

Section One — Number

Rounding Decimals

1) You might need to round decimal numbers to make them whole numbers. For example, if the question is about money (£ or p) or measurements (m, km, kg).

2) Look at the first digit after the decimal point.

3) If it's less than 5, round the number down.

4) If it's 5 or more, round the number up.

Example 1

Ramesh is buying some material. It costs 232.4p per metre. How much is this to the nearest pence?

Look at the first digit after the decimal point.

4 is less than 5, so round down.

The material costs **232p** per metre to the nearest pence.

Example 2

Some sweets cost £3.50 per kg. How much do they cost to the nearest pound?

The first digit after the decimal point is a 5, so you need to round up.

The sweets cost **£4** per kg to the nearest pound.

Practice Questions

1) Tom has 134 red pens.

   a) How many pens does Tom have to the nearest 10?

   ....

   b) How many pens does Tom have to the nearest 100?

   ....

2) Alex has 550 fax machines. How many does he have to the nearest 100?

   ....

3) Cheese costs £6.26 per kg. How much is this to the nearest pound (£)?

   ....

Estimating

Estimating Uses Rounding

1) An estimate is a close guess at what an answer will be.
2) You can use rounding to estimate an answer.

Example

Kyle has 32 fairy cakes and 118 cup cakes.
Estimate how many cakes Kyle has in total.

See pages 22-23 for more on rounding.

1) First round both numbers to the nearest 10.

   32 rounds down to 30.

   118 rounds up to 120.

2) Then add 30 and 120: 120 + 30 = 150

   So Kyle has about **150 cakes** in total.

Estimating Money Calculations

Example

Carl is buying supplies on the company credit card.
So far he has spent £15.99, £13.99, and £127.99.
Estimate how much he has spent so far.

1) First round all the numbers to the nearest £1.

   £15.99 rounds up to £16.

   £13.99 rounds up to £14.

   £127.99 rounds up to £128.

2) Then add them together: 16 + 14 + 128 = £158.00

   So Carl has spent about **£158.00** so far.

Section One — Number

Estimating Sizes

You might need to estimate the size of one thing when given the size of something else.

Example

Ajit's dining room table is 2 m long. Use the images on the right to estimate the length of his coffee table.

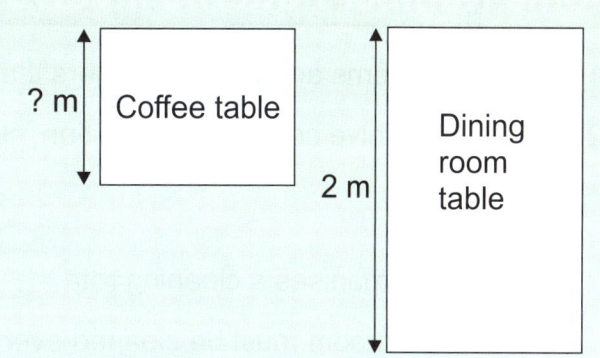

The coffee table looks about $\frac{1}{2}$ the length of the dining room table.

$\frac{1}{2} \times 2 = 1 \div 2 \times 2 = 1$ m. Ajit's coffee table is about **1 m** long.

Practice Questions

1) Estimate the answer to 617 + 84.

   ....

2) Caz is doing some stock taking. She has 98 tins of beans, 45 tins of tomatoes, and 23 tins of spaghetti. Estimate how many tins she has in total.

   ....

3) Anna-Lee has collected £38 for charity in a spare change box from one local cafe. She has boxes in 17 places in total. Estimate how much she might have collected in total.

   ....

4) Racquel is shopping. She buys food costing £1.99, £2.99, 99p, 99p and £3.99. She pays with a £20 note. Estimate how much change she'll get.

   ....

5) The height of the ladder is 3 m.
   Use the diagram to estimate how tall the building is.

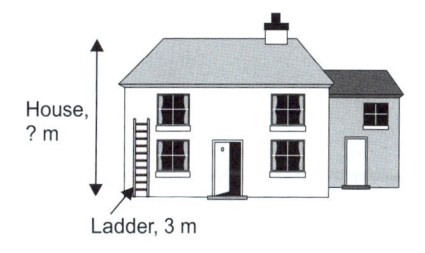

   ....

Section One — Number

Number Patterns

Some Number Patterns Involve Counting

1) Number patterns are lists of numbers that follow a pattern.

2) They can involve counting, or addition, subtraction, multiplication or division.

Example

Darryl organises a cleaning rota.

The bathroom must be cleaned every 5 days.

It has been cleaned on Tuesday in week 1.

Mark in the next 3 times the bathroom should be cleaned.

Week 1	Week 2	Week 3
Monday	Monday	Monday
Tuesday *bathroom*	Tuesday	Tuesday
Wednesday	Wednesday	Wednesday
Thursday	Thursday	Thursday
Friday	Friday	Friday
Saturday	Saturday	Saturday
Sunday	Sunday	Sunday

The bathroom needs to be cleaned every 5 days.

From Tuesday, count on 5 days — that's the next day it needs to be cleaned. So the next day it needs to be cleaned is Sunday in week 1. Then count on 5 days from here and so on.

So the bathroom should be cleaned on...

- Sunday of week 1.
- Friday of week 2.
- Wednesday of week 3.

Section One — Number

Number Patterns Involving Multiplication and Division

Example 1

Flo has some shares in a company. They double in value each month.
In January they are worth £35.
How much are the shares worth at the end of March?

Double just means multiply by 2 (× 2). Triple means multiply by 3 (× 3).

The pattern here is × 2 for each month until March.

January = £35

February = £35 × 2 = £70

March = £70 × 2 = £140

At the end of March the shares are worth **£140**.

Example 2

There is a sale on in Josie's shop. She is trying to sell half her stock of crisps every hour. She has 16 boxes.
How many boxes will she have left after 3 hours?

Halving something is the same as dividing it by 2.

The pattern here is ÷ 2 every hour for 3 hours.

1 hour, 16 ÷ 2 = 8 boxes,
2 hours, 8 ÷ 2 = 4 boxes,   ← *Divide the previous answer by 2 each time.*
3 hours, 4 ÷ 2 = 2 boxes.

After 3 hours Josie has **2 boxes** left.

Practice Questions

1) Lloyd went to the doctors on the 10th Oct. He was prescribed some tablets to be taken every 4 days starting that day. On which dates in October does Lloyd need to take the tablets?

....

....

....

October						
1	2	3	4	5	6	7
8	9	10 *Dr's app*	11	12	13	14
15	16	17	18	19	20 *Hair*	21
22	23	24	25	26	27 *Dinner?*	28
29	30 *Chris Bday*	31				

2) Willow is growing some bacteria. She has 15 bacteria to start with. They double in number every hour. How many will she have in 4 hours?

....

Section One — Number

Units

Everything You Measure Has Units

1) When you measure something you need to give the units.

2) Units tell you what type of number you've got. For example, you can't just say that a distance is 4 — you need to know if it's 4 metres or 4 miles.

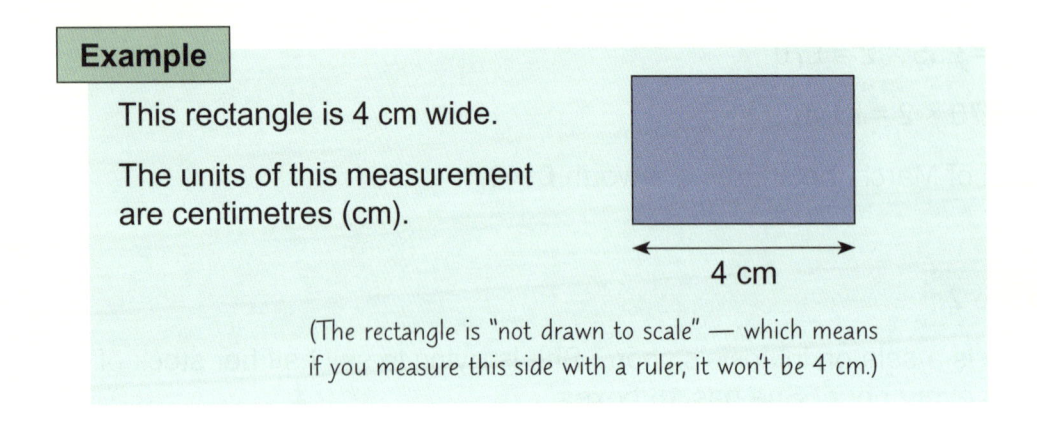

Example

This rectangle is 4 cm wide.

The units of this measurement are centimetres (cm).

4 cm

(The rectangle is "not drawn to scale" — which means if you measure this side with a ruler, it won't be 4 cm.)

Units of Length

1) Length is how long something is.

2) Common units of length are:
   - millimetres (mm)
   - centimetres (cm)
   - metres (m)
   - kilometres (km)

3) Here's how some of these units are related:

This means that 1 cm is the same as 10 mm.
Another way of saying this is that there are 10 mm in 1 cm.

Length
1 cm = 10 mm
1 m = 100 cm
1 km = 1000 m

4) You might also see length measured in feet and inches. For example, these units are sometimes used to give someone's height.

Section Two — Measure

Units of Weight

1) Weight is how heavy something is.

2) Common units of weight are:
   - grams (g)
   - kilograms (kg)

3) Here's how these units are related:

   Weight
   1 kg = 1000 g

4) You might also see weight measured in stones or pounds.
   For example, these units are sometimes used to give a person's weight.

Units of Capacity

1) Capacity is how much something will hold.
   For example, how much liquid a jug will hold.

2) Common units of capacity are:
   - millilitres (ml)
   - centilitres (cl)
   - litres (L)

3) Here's how some of these units are related:

   Capacity
   1 cl = 10 ml
   1 L = 100 cl (or 1000 ml)

4) You might also see capacity measured in pints.
   For example, the capacity of a milk bottle is often measured in pints.

Section Two — Measure

Practice Questions

1) Circle the unit of length: metre   kilogram   centilitre

2) Circle the unit of weight: centimetre   gram   litre

3) Circle the unit of capacity: millilitre   kilometre   gram

4) Underline the units in the following sentences:

    a) An antique clock is 1.7 metres tall and 40 centimetres wide.

    b) A cardboard box weighs 200 g. When it's filled with books it weighs 14 kg.

    c) A barrel contains 160 litres of oil.

5) How many metres are in a kilometre?

    ....

6) How many grams are in a kilogram?

    ....

7) How many centilitres are in a litre?

    ....

8) In the following pairs, circle the unit that is bigger.

    a) millimetre or centimetre

    b) kilometre or metre

    c) centilitre or millilitre

Length

Length is How Long Something is

You might have to answer questions where you have to do calculations with lengths.

Example 1

Colette has a 1.5 m length of fabric. She buys another 1 m long piece. What is the total length of fabric Colette has now?

To find the total length, add together the lengths of the two pieces:

Total length = 1.5 m + 1 m = 2.5 m

So Colette has **2.5 m** of fabric.

Example 2

Matthew needs to paint a line halfway along a football pitch. The pitch is 100 m long. Where should Matthew paint the line?

To find out where halfway along the pitch is, divide the length of the pitch by 2:

Halfway along the pitch = 100 m ÷ 2 = 50 m

So Matthew needs to paint the line at **50 m**.

Practice Questions

1) Anna has covered 4 km on her run. If she carries on for another 2 km, how far will she have run in total?

   ....

2) Simon is painting his garden fence. The fence is 80 m long. So far he has painted 45 m. How much does he have left to paint?

   ....

3) Andy has three planks of wood. Two planks are each 1.5 m long. One plank is 2.5 m long. What is the total length of all three planks?

   ....

Section Two — Measure

Changing from One Unit to Another

1) If a number has units after it, then you can only add or take away, or divide or multiply by another number with the same units.

2) So to answer some questions, you might need to change from one unit to another.

3) You can use the tables on pages 28 and 29 to help you change between different units.

   This table will help you change between units of length:

Length
1 cm = 10 mm
1 m = 100 cm
1 km = 1000 m

   You won't get tables like this in your test, so you'll need to learn them.

Example

Calvin's ladder is 2 m long. He extends it by 110 cm. How long is the ladder now?

You need to add 110 cm to 2 m, but you can't because the units are different.

So first you need to change one of the lengths, so that they both have the same units.

You can see from the table that 1 m = 100 cm. So to change m into cm you multiply by 100:

Length
1 cm = 10 mm
1 m = 100 cm
1 km = 1000 m

2 m × 100 = 200 cm

Now the units are all the same (cm), you can add the two lengths together:

200 cm + 110 cm = 310 cm.

So Calvin's ladder is **310 cm** long when it's extended.

Practice Questions

1) Marie is building a wall. It is 1.5 m high. Marie wants to add another 50 cm to the wall. How high will the wall be when Marie has finished it?

   ....

   ....

2) Virginie is making a bracelet by putting beads on a string. Each bead is 5 mm wide. The string is 14 cm long. How many beads can Virginie fit on the string?

   ....

   ....

Section Two — Measure

Comparing Lengths

Sometimes you might have to compare lengths (or widths, or heights).

Example

A basketball team is looking for a new player.

The heights of five possible players are shown in the table.

Player	Height
1	1.89 m
2	1.92 m
3	1.98 m
4	1.80 m
5	2.00 m

1) The team want a player who is at least 1.90 m tall. Which players could they choose?

   You need to look for players who are 1.90 m or more.
   - Player 1 is only 1.89 m, so he is too small.
   - Player 4 is only 1.80 m, so he is also too small.

   Players 2, 3 and 5 are all over 1.90 m. So the basketball team could choose any of these players.

2) The team decide to choose the tallest player they can. Which player should they choose?

   Player 5 is 2 m tall. This makes him the tallest player. So they should choose player 5.

Practice Question

1) Tony wants to buy a rug. The rug needs to be:
   - at least 1.8 m long
   - no longer than 2.7 m.

   Which of the following rugs could Tony choose?

Rug	1	2	3	4	5
Length	1.9 m	2.9 m	2.6 m	1.5 m	2.6 m

Section Two — Measure

Estimating Lengths

In your test, you might be asked to estimate how long something needs to be.

Example

At a wedding there will be 6 people sat along one side of the top table. Estimate how long the table needs to be.

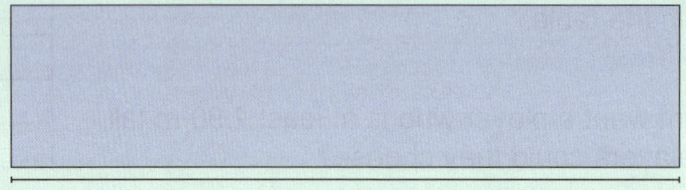

?

1) First you need to decide how much space each person will need. This means making a sensible guess.

   To do this it helps to think of an object you already know the length of. For example, a 30 cm ruler.

   1 ruler length isn't really enough space for someone to eat a meal in.

   But 2 ruler lengths is a bit better.

   30 cm × 2 = 60 cm
   So each person needs about 60 cm of space.

2) To work out the length the table needs to be, you need to multiply the amount of space each person needs by 6:

   60 cm × 6 = 360 cm

   So the table needs to be at least **360 cm** long.

Practice Question

1) A row of 8 parking spaces need to be made for some new flats. Estimate how long the row of parking spaces needs to be.

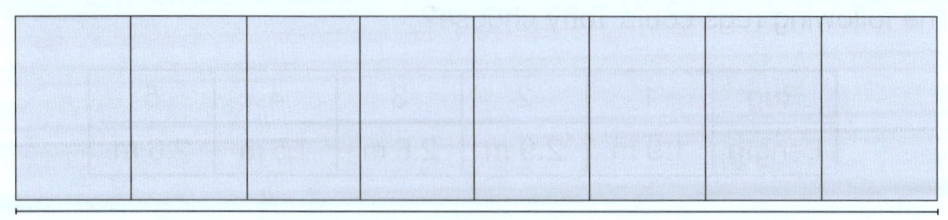

   ? m

   ....
   ....

Section Two — Measure

Perimeter

Finding the Perimeter

The perimeter is the distance around the outside of a shape.

To find a perimeter, you add up the lengths of all the sides.

Example 1

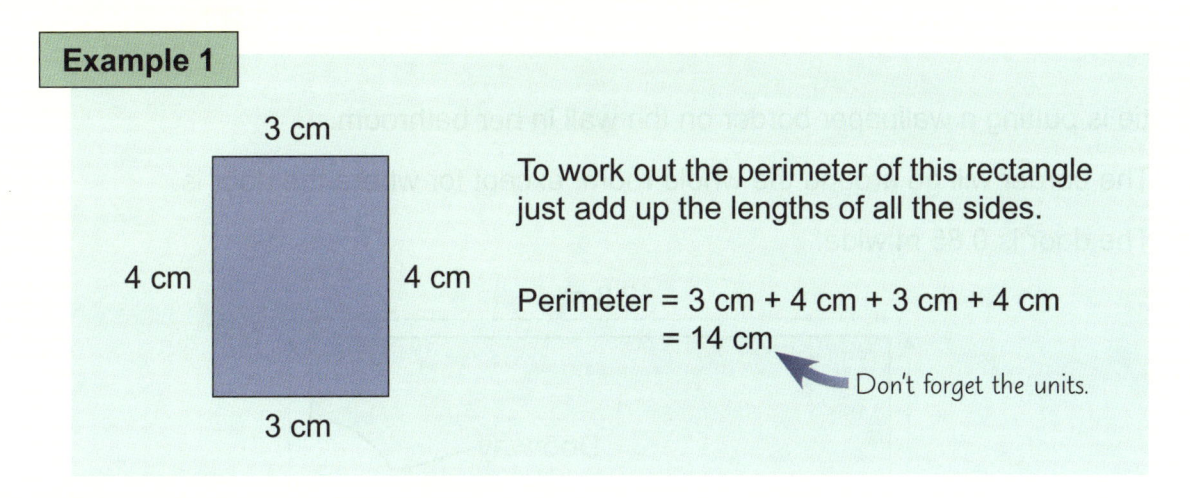

3 cm
4 cm
4 cm
3 cm

To work out the perimeter of this rectangle just add up the lengths of all the sides.

Perimeter = 3 cm + 4 cm + 3 cm + 4 cm
= 14 cm

Don't forget the units.

Example 2

Fiona wants to put some wire fencing around her chicken run.

The diagram below shows the chicken run.

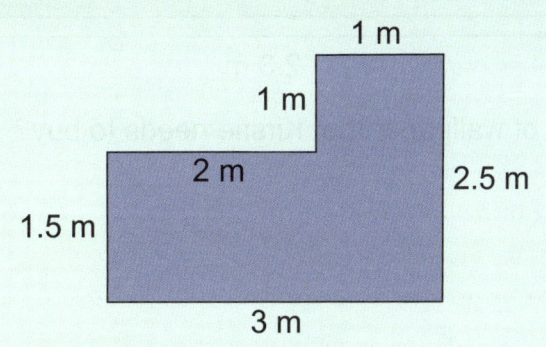

1 m
1 m
2 m
2.5 m
1.5 m
3 m

How much fencing does Fiona need to buy?

The fencing will go all the way around the outside of the chicken run. So to answer this question, you need to work out the perimeter of the chicken run.

Write down the lengths of all the sides of the run and add them together.

Perimeter = 1.5 m + 2 m + 1 m + 1 m + 2.5 m + 3 m = 11 m

So Fiona needs to buy **11 m** of fencing.

Practice Questions

1) Find the perimeter of the shape on the right.

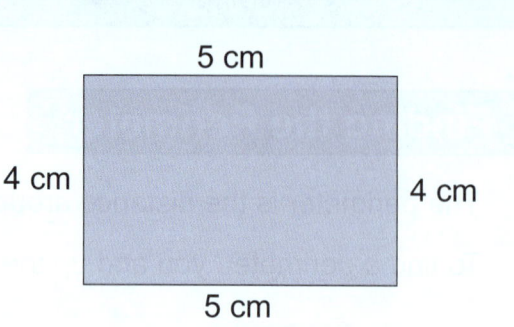

   ....

   ....

   5 cm
   4 cm   4 cm
   5 cm

2) Kirstie is putting a wallpaper border on the wall in her bathroom.
   - The border will go around the whole room, except for where the door is.
   - The door is 0.85 m wide.

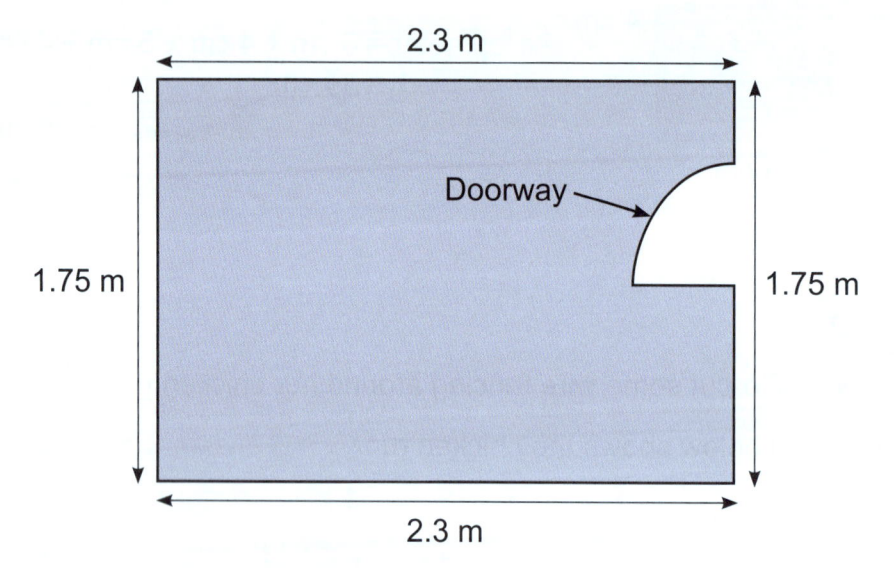

   2.3 m
   1.75 m   Doorway   1.75 m
   2.3 m

   What is the total length of wallpaper that Kirstie needs to buy?

   ....

   ....

   ....

   ....

   ....

Section Two — Measure

Weight

Weight is How Heavy Something is

You need to be able to solve problems involving weight.

Example 1

Aiden fills a box with books and board games.
The books weigh 4.5 kg. The board games weigh 2.5 kg.
The empty box weighs 0.2 kg. How much does the filled box weigh?

Add up the weights of the books, the board games and the empty box:

4.5 kg + 2.5 kg + 0.2 kg = 7.2 kg

So the filled box weighs **7.2 kg**.

Example 2

A sack of potatoes weighs 25 kg. Alan's trailer can carry a maximum of 240 kg.
He needs to transport 14 sacks of potatoes. Can he do this in 1 trip?

First, work out the weight of 14 sacks of potatoes.
To do this multiply 25 kg by 14:

25 kg × 14 = 350 kg

350 kg is more than the maximum weight Alan's trailer can carry (240 kg).
So Alan **can't** transport all 14 sacks in 1 trip.

Example 3

Ellie buys a 1.5 kg bag of muesli. She buys a 450 g box of muesli too.
What is the total weight of muesli Ellie has bought?

First you need to change one of the weights, so they both have the same units.

Remember, 1 kg = 1000 g.
So to change kg to g you multiply by 1000.

1.5 kg × 1000 = 1500 g

Weight
1 kg = 1000 g

This table is also on p. 29.

Now the units are all the same (g), you can add the two weights together:

1500 g + 450 g = 1950 g.

So the muesli weighs **1950 g** in total.

Section Two — Measure

Practice Questions

1) Sunaira recently lost 5.5 kg in weight. Before this she weighed 78 kg. How much does she weigh now?

....

2) Paul needs to carry 5 bags to his car. Each bag weighs 5 kg. Paul can safely carry 20 kg in one go. How many bags can he carry in one go?

....

....

3) Harriet buys 1 kg of pasta. She uses 350 g for a recipe. How much does she have left?

....

....

Comparing Weights

It's often useful to compare the different weights of things.
For example, if you want to work out the heaviest or lightest thing in a group.

Example

Melissa, Sam and Jo need to find a fourth person for their rowing team.
The team can't weigh more than 228 kg in total.
The three of them currently weigh 167 kg.

Who should they ask to be their fourth member?

Person	Weight (kg)
Lucy	58
Rachel	68
Clare	62
Kate	63

1) Work out the amount of weight they have left over for a fourth member:

   Weight left over = 228 kg − 167 kg = 61 kg

2) So the fourth member needs to weigh 61 kg or less.
   The only person in the table that weighs less than 61 kg is Lucy.

They should ask **Lucy** to be their fourth member.

Section Two — Measure

Estimating Weights

You might need to estimate the weight of something in your test.

Example

Brad buys the following items at a supermarket:

Apples — 0.9 kg, Potatoes — 1.2 kg, Carrots — 1.15 kg

Estimate the weight of Brad's shopping.

Round each weight up or down to give a whole number.
Then add all 3 weights together.

0.9 kg rounds up to 1 kg. 1.2 kg and 1.15 kg both round down to 1 kg.

So each group of items weighs about 1 kg.

1 + 1 + 1 = 3 kg

So Brad's shopping weighs about 3 kg.

Practice Questions

1) Liz is going backpacking. She wants to buy the lightest sleeping bag she can. Look at the table. Which sleeping bag should Liz buy?

Sleeping bag	Weight (g)
Sleep Right XV	1160
Comfort Pro VII	1400
Sleeper Light	800
Travelmaster 3000	1000

....

2) Dennis is on a low fat diet.
Which of the following sandwiches would be the best choice for his lunch?

Sandwich	Fat (g)
Chicken Mayonnaise	15.2
Tuna Mayonnaise	12.2
Ham and egg salad	13.5

....

3) Paula weighs 55.2 kg. Louise weighs 59.6 kg. Estimate how much the two weigh in total.

....

....

Section Two — Measure

Capacity

Volume and Capacity

Volume is the amount of space something takes up.

Capacity is how much something will hold.

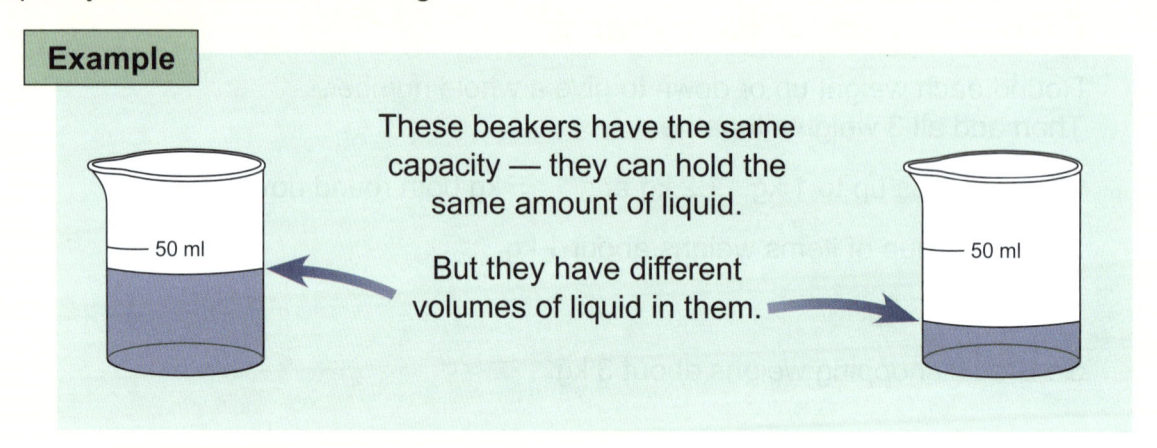

Example

These beakers have the same capacity — they can hold the same amount of liquid.

But they have different volumes of liquid in them.

Questions on Capacity and Volume

You need to be able to answer questions involving capacity and volume.

Example 1

Jodie showers twice a day. Each shower uses about 45 litres of water. How much water does Jodie use showering each week?

Each day Jodie uses: 45 litres × 2 = 90 litres of water

In a week, Jodie uses 7 times this amount: 90 litres × 7 = 630 litres

So Jodie uses **630 litres** of water for showering each week.

Example 2

Mark is filling a 65 litre fish tank using a 5 litre bucket.
How many full buckets of water will it take to fill the tank completely?

Divide the capacity of the tank by the capacity of the bucket.

65 ÷ 5 = 13

So, **13 full buckets** of water would fill the tank.

Section Two — Measure

> **Example 3**
>
> Gareth has made 5 L of stock.
> How many 500 ml measuring jugs can he fill with the stock?
>
> You need to divide 5 L by 500 ml, but you can't because the units are different.
>
> So first you need to change one of the measurements so the units are the same.
>
> Remember, 1 L = 1000 ml.
> So to change L to ml you multiply by 1000.
>
> 5 L × 1000 = 5000 ml
>
> | Capacity |
> |---|
> | 1 cl = 10 ml |
> | 1 L = 100 cl (or 1000 ml) |
>
> Now the units are all the same (ml), you can divide the amount of stock by the capacity of a measuring jug.
>
> 5000 ml ÷ 500 ml = 10
>
> So Gareth can fill **10 measuring jugs** with the stock.

Practice Questions

1) A 500 ml bottle is filled with 200 ml of water.

    a) What is the capacity of the bottle? ....

    b) What is the volume of water in the bottle? ....

2) Gary has bought a fountain. It takes him three full 2.5 litre buckets of water to fill it. How much water is in the fountain?

    ....

3) Catherine is going cycling with 3 friends. They take 2 L of water for each person. At the end of the day they have 0.8 L of water left. How much water have they drunk?

    ....

    ....

4) A jug is filled with 1 litre of orange juice. Four 200 ml glasses are poured from the jug. How much orange juice is left in the jug?

    ....

    ....

Section Two — Measure

Comparing Volumes or Capacities

You might need to compare different volumes or capacities in your test.

Example

Hannah uses about 4.5 L of water to water her vegetables. Which watering can is the best for Hannah to use?

Watering can	Capacity
1	5 L
2	4 L
3	10 L

The capacity of watering can 2 is too low — 4 L is less than 4.5 L, so Hannah would need to fill the can more than once.

The capacity of watering can 3 is too big. It holds much more than Hannah needs. It'd probably be quite hard to carry.

Watering can 1 seems like the best can to use. It can hold 5 L of water. This is just over the 4.5 L Hannah needs to water her vegetables.

Estimating Volumes or Capacities

For some problems you might need to estimate volumes or capacities.

Example

The beakers below are the same size. Beaker 1 contains 200 ml of liquid. Estimate the volume of liquid in beaker 2.

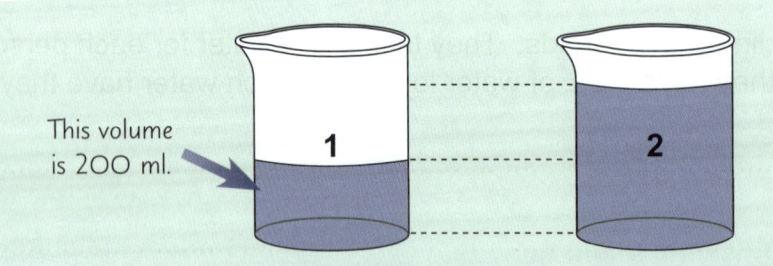

This volume is 200 ml.

1) Compare the volume of liquid in each beaker.

2) It looks like there's twice as much liquid in beaker 2 than in beaker 1.

$$200 \text{ ml} \times 2 = 400 \text{ ml}.$$

So there's probably about **400 ml** of liquid in the beaker 2.

Section Two — Measure

Practice Questions

1) Charlie is having a new hot water tank fitted in his guest house.
He wants it to have a capacity of over 160 L.

Hot water tank	Capacity
Duchess XL	150 L
Herald 175	175 L
Issigo ZF	130 L
AEB 224	165 L

Which of the tanks in the table above could he have fitted?

....

2) Sue wants to buy a small bottle of shampoo to take on holiday. The bottle can have a maximum capacity of 100 ml. She finds 3 bottles she could buy: 85 ml, 125 ml and 50 ml.

Sue wants to buy the biggest bottle she can. Which one should she buy?

....

3) The bottles below each have a capacity of 1000 ml.
Estimate the volume of liquid in each one.

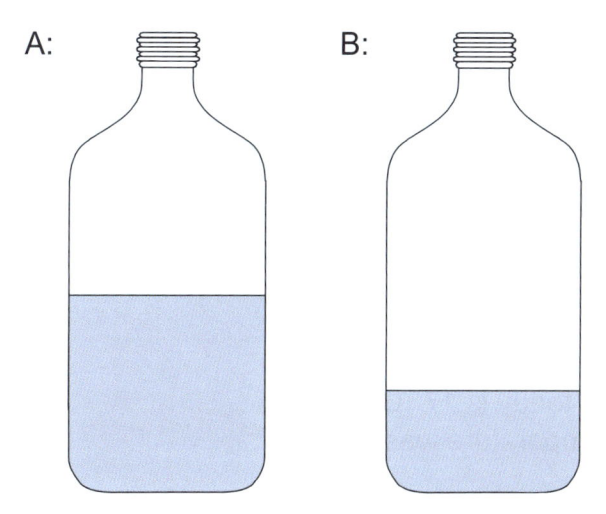

A:

B:

Volume of liquid in bottle A: ....

Volume of liquid in bottle B: ....

Section Two — Measure

Temperature

Temperature is How Hot or Cold it is

1) Temperature is a number that shows how hot or cold something is.

2) An object with a high temperature is warm or hot. For example, the inside of an oven.

3) An object with a low temperature is cool or cold. For example, the inside of a fridge.

4) Temperature can have different units.
   The most common are called degrees Celsius (°C).

Examples

The temperature in a normal oven can reach around 230 °C.

The temperature on a summer's day in the UK might be 26 °C.

The temperature in a fridge is usually around 5 °C.

Water turns to ice at 0 °C.

Calculations Involving Temperature

You might be asked to work out the difference between two temperatures.

Example

The temperature today is 17 °C.
Yesterday the temperature was 14 °C.

What is the difference in temperature between today and yesterday?

To find the difference, subtract the smaller temperature from the larger one.

17 °C – 14 °C = 3 °C

So the difference in temperature is **3 °C**.

Section Two — Measure

Comparing Different Temperatures

It is often useful to compare different temperatures.

Example

The Parker family want to go on a day trip to the coast.
The table shows the temperature forecast for 3 different places.

The Parkers want to visit the place that's likely to be warmest. Where should they go?

	Temperature (° C)
Sandy Head	20
Minkie Bay	23
Port Anne	19

You need to find the place with the highest temperature in the table.
The table shows that Minkie Bay has the highest temperature (23 °C).

So the Parkers should visit **Minkie Bay**.

Practice Questions

1) Circle the highest temperature: 27 °C   38 °C   21 °C

2) Circle the lowest temperature: 2 °C   0 °C   5 °C

3) The temperature in Jeff's flat on Monday morning was 18.5 °C.
   On Tuesday morning it was 17 °C.

   a) What is the difference in temperature between the two mornings?

   ....

   b) On which morning was it warmest?

   ....

4) Caitlin has 3 recipes for biscuits. One says to set the oven to 200 °C, another says 190 °C and the final recipe says 225 °C. Caitlin decides to set the oven to the lowest temperature. Which temperature is this?

   ....

Section Two — Measure

Estimating Temperatures

You might need to estimate the temperature of something.

Example

At a leisure centre, the temperature in the gym is about 20 °C.
The water in the jacuzzi is about 40 °C.
Estimate the temperature inside the sauna.

You need to use the information you're given to come up with a sensible answer here.

It's twice as warm in the jacuzzi as it is in the gym.

It could be twice as warm in the sauna as it is in the jacuzzi.
(Saunas are very hot.)

40 °C × 2 = 80 °C

So the temperature in the sauna could be around 80 °C.

This isn't the only right answer here — the point is to make a sensible guess. For example: the sauna probably isn't colder than the gym — so a guess of 10 °C wouldn't be very sensible.

Practice Question

1) In January, the average temperature in Keith's garden was 6 °C. In May, it was 14 °C. August was the hottest month — the average temperature was 24 °C

   Estimate the temperature in Keith's garden in each of the following months:

   a) March

   b) July

Section Two — Measure

Scales

Scales are Used to Measure Things

1) A scale is something that you use to measure things.

2) Scales are found on things like rulers, kitchen scales, measuring jugs and thermometers.

Measuring Length

You can use the scale on a ruler to measure length.

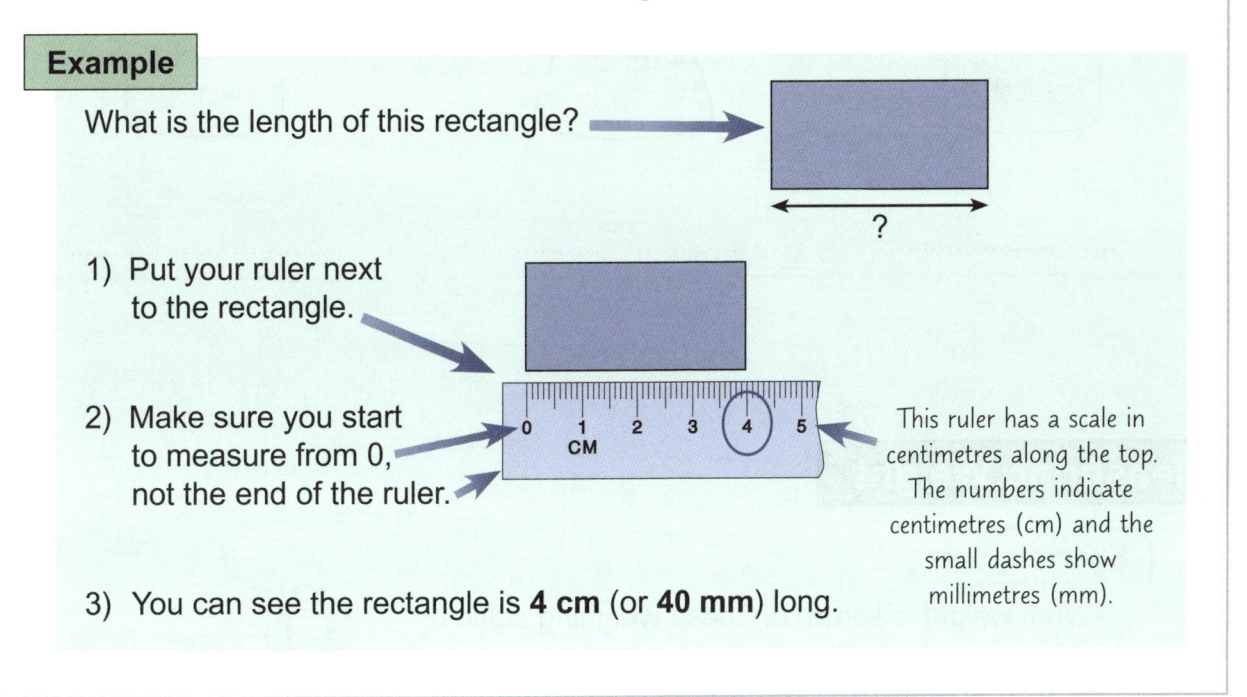

Example

What is the length of this rectangle?

1) Put your ruler next to the rectangle.

2) Make sure you start to measure from 0, not the end of the ruler.

This ruler has a scale in centimetres along the top. The numbers indicate centimetres (cm) and the small dashes show millimetres (mm).

3) You can see the rectangle is **4 cm** (or **40 mm**) long.

Measuring Volume

You can use the scale on a measuring cylinder to measure volume.

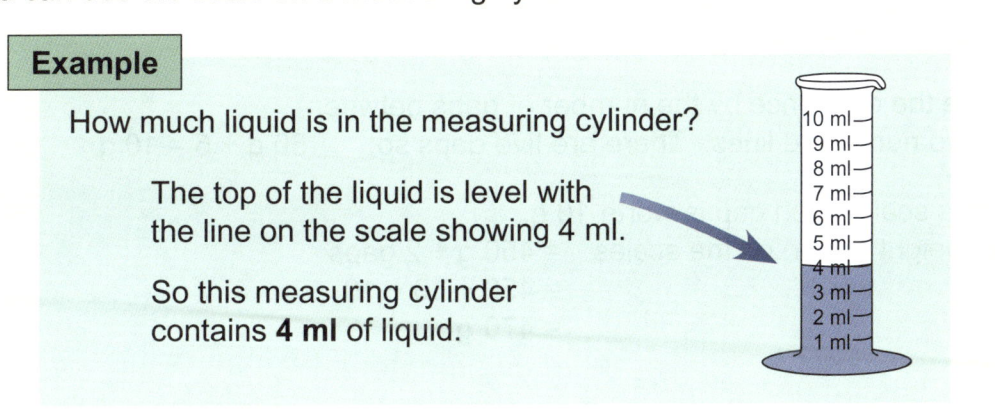

Example

How much liquid is in the measuring cylinder?

The top of the liquid is level with the line on the scale showing 4 ml.

So this measuring cylinder contains **4 ml** of liquid.

Section Two — Measure

Practice Questions

1) Give the length of one side of the square on the right.

   ....

   ....

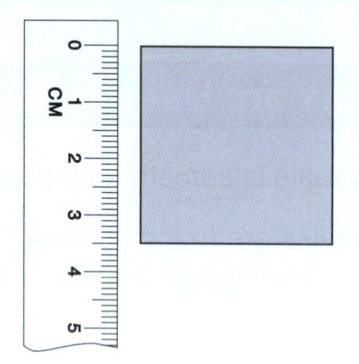

2) How much liquid is in the following containers?

   a)   b)   c)

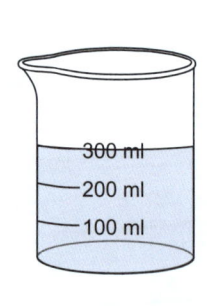

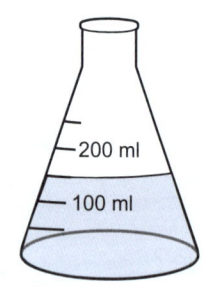

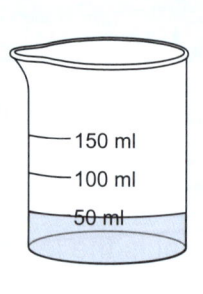

   ....

Measuring Weight

Example

What weight is shown on these weighing scales?

The arrow points to the weight in grams.

It points to a line with no number, so you'll need to work out what weight it's showing.

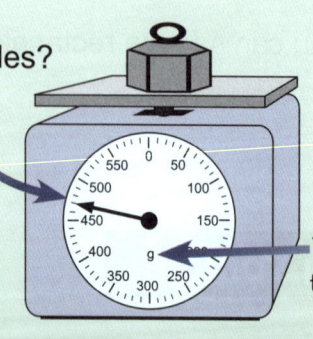

To work this out:

1) Find the difference between the two numbered lines on either side of the arrow: 500 g − 450 g = 50 g

2) Divide the difference by the number of gaps between the two numbered lines. There are five gaps so: 50 g ÷ 5 = 10 g

So on this scale, each gap is worth 10 g.
So, the weight shown on the scales   = 450 g + 2 gaps
  = 450 + 10 + 10
  = **470 g**

This g shows that the scales measure in grams (g).

Section Two — Measure

Measuring Temperature

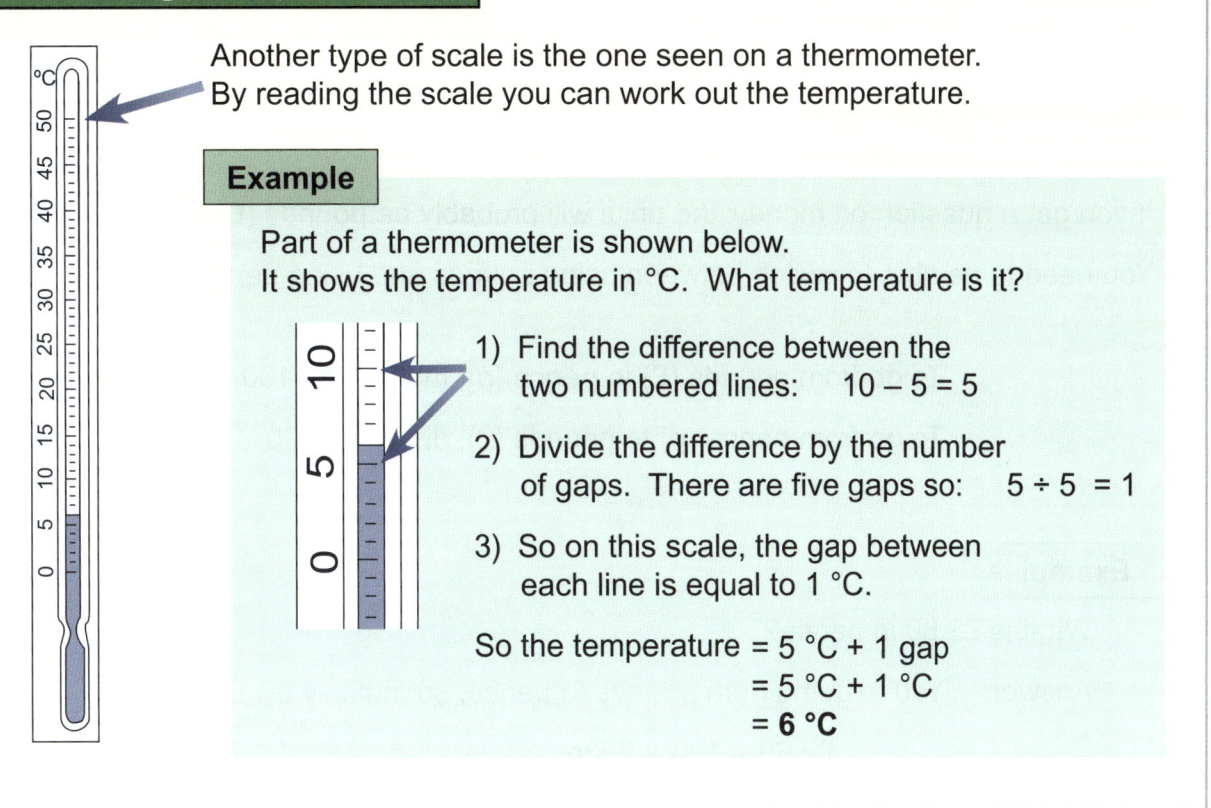

Another type of scale is the one seen on a thermometer. By reading the scale you can work out the temperature.

Example

Part of a thermometer is shown below. It shows the temperature in °C. What temperature is it?

1) Find the difference between the two numbered lines: 10 − 5 = 5

2) Divide the difference by the number of gaps. There are five gaps so: 5 ÷ 5 = 1

3) So on this scale, the gap between each line is equal to 1 °C.

So the temperature = 5 °C + 1 gap
= 5 °C + 1 °C
= **6 °C**

Practice Questions

1) Every day, Anna records the temperature in her conservatory. The thermometer on the right shows the temperature one morning in °C.

   What temperature is shown on the thermometer?

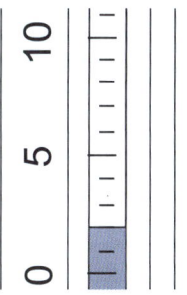

   ....

   ....

2) On the right is the dial from a set of weighing scales.

   What is the weight shown?

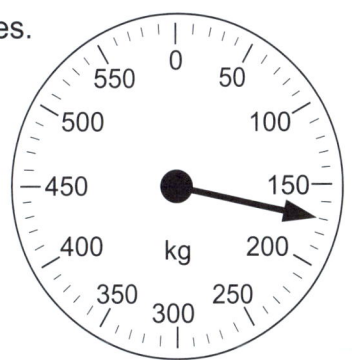

   ....

   ....

   ....

Section Two — Measure

Money

Pounds and Pence

1) If you get a question on money, the units will probably be pounds (£) or pence (p).

2) You need to be able to switch between using pounds and using pence.

> To go from pounds (£) to pence (p), multiply by 100.
>
> To go from pence (p) to pounds (£), divide by 100.

Examples

What is £2.60 in pence?

Answer: You're going from pounds to pence, so multiply by 100.

$$£2.60 \times 100 = 260p$$

What is 76p in pounds?

Answer: You're going from pence to pounds, so divide by 100.

$$76p \div 100 = £0.76$$

Use Pounds OR Pence in Calculations — Not Both

1) You may get a question that uses pounds and pence.

2) If you do, you'll need to change the units so that they're all in pounds or all in pence.

Example

Cian buys a DVD online for £7.49. He pays 99p for postage. How much has he spent in total?

1) Change the price of the postage from pence to pounds.

$$99p \div 100 = £0.99$$

2) Both prices are now in the same units (£). So add together the cost of the DVD and the postage.

$$£7.49 + £0.99 = £8.48$$

So Cian has spent £8.48.

Practice Questions

1) a) What is £3.84 in pence? b) What is £1.27 in pence?

2) a) What is 61p in pounds (£)? b) What is 231p in pounds (£)?

3) Which is more expensive, a pen that costs 65p or one that costs £0.69?

4) Steph is buying a box of cereal bars that cost £1.98. She has a voucher for 50p off. How much will Steph pay?

5) Grace has been shopping. She bought bread for £1.20, milk for 90p and eggs for £1.45. What was the total cost of her shopping? Give your answer in pounds (£).

More Calculations Involving Money

There are lots of different types of calculations you can do with money.

Example 1

Will is looking at two TVs in a shop. One costs £259 and the other costs £324. What is the price difference between the two TVs?

Answer:

You need to subtract the smaller price from the larger one.

Price difference: £324 − £259 = £65

So there is a £65 price difference between the two TVs.

Section Two — Measure

> **Example 2**
>
> Keri buys 2 cakes for £3. How much would it cost her to buy 5 cakes?
>
> 1) First you need to work out how much 1 cake costs.
>   You know that 2 cakes cost £3, so you need to divide £3 by 2.
>
>   Cost of 1 cake: £3 ÷ 2 = £1.50
>
> 2) Now multiply the price of 1 cake by 5.
>
>   Cost of 5 cakes: £1.50 × 5 = £7.50
>
> So it would cost Keri **£7.50** to buy 5 cakes.

> **Example 3**
>
> Sabrina would like to buy a newspaper for £1.20, a packet of crisps for 55p and birthday card for £2.40. She has £4.20 in her purse.
> Does she have enough money to buy all 3 things?
>
> 1) First, you need to change all the prices into the same units.
>   So change the price of the crisps from pence to pounds.
>
>   55p ÷ 100 = £0.55
>
>   *See page 50 for help changing pence to pounds.*
>
> 2) Now add up the cost of all 3 things.
>
>   £1.20 + £0.55 + £2.40 = £4.15
>
> The cost of the 3 things is £4.15. Sabrina has £4.20 in her purse.
> £4.20 is more than £4.15, so **yes** she has enough money to buy all 3 things.

Practice Questions

1) James is buying some pet fish. He buys 4 angelfish for £18.
   How much would it cost him to buy 5 fish?

   ....

   ....

2) Janice is having a dinner party. She wants to spend £30 on food, £25 on drinks and £10 on decorations. She has an overall budget of £60. Can she afford to spend what she wants?

   ....

   ....

Section Two — Measure

Value for Money Calculations

1) If you're buying a pack of something, you can work out how much you're paying for each item.

   Price per item = total price ÷ number of items

2) You can then compare the price per item for that pack with other packs.

Example

A shop sells tins of sweetcorn in packs of 3 or 6. The 3-pack costs £1.50. The 6-pack costs £2.70.

3-pack: Price per tin = £1.50 ÷ 3 = £0.50

6-pack: Price per tin = £2.70 ÷ 6 = £0.45

Price per tin = total price ÷ number of tins

The 6-pack costs less per tin, so it's better value than the 3-pack.

3) You can also compare costs by looking at how much you'd pay per gram of something.

   Price per gram = total price ÷ number of grams

Example

A 340 g tin of sweetcorn costs 82p. A 200 g tin of sweetcorn costs 60p.

340 g tin: Price per gram = 82p ÷ 340 = 0.24p

200 g tin: Price per gram = 60p ÷ 200 = 0.3p

The 340 g tin costs less per gram, so it's better value than the 200 g tin.

Practice Questions

1) At a bakery you can buy 6 bread rolls for £2. At a different bakery you can get 8 bread rolls for £2.40. Which deal is the best value for money?

   ....

   ....

2) A 450 g tin of treacle costs 72p. A 750 g tin of treacle costs 135p. Which is the best value for money?

   ....

   ....

Calendars

Calendars Show the Date

1) Calendars show all of the days, weeks and months in a year.

2) A calendar for the month of October is shown below.

OCTOBER

MON	TUES	WED	THURS	FRI	SAT	SUN
		1	2	3	4	5
6	7	8	9	10	11	12
13	14	15	16	17	18	19
20	21	22	23	24	25	26
27	28	29	30	31		

The days of the week are along the top. Either Sunday or Monday comes first.

Each line of numbers shows the dates for one week.

You can see from the calendar that the 5th of October is a Sunday.

Working Out Dates Using a Calendar

You might be asked questions where you need to look at calendars and work out dates.

Example 1

Dave has ordered a new dining table. It is being delivered on the second Thursday in April.

On what date is Dave's table being delivered?

APRIL

MON	TUES	WED	THURS	FRI	SAT	SUN
					1	2
3	4	5	6	7	8	9
10	11	12	13	14	15	16
17	18	19	20	21	22	23
24	25	26	27	28	29	30

1) First, find the day along the top of the calendar.
   Thursday is the 4th day along. The dates below it (in the blue box on the calendar) are the dates of every Thursday in the month.

2) Now count down to the second date.
   This is the second Thursday of the month — the 13th.

So Dave's table will be delivered on the 13th of April.

Example 2

Karen wants to go on holiday with her sister Ruth for a weekend in March.

March						
Sun	Mon	Tues	Wed	Thurs	Fri	Sat
		1	2	3	4	5
6	7	8	9	10	11	12
13	14	15	16	17	18	19
20	21	22	23	24	25	26
27	28	29	30	31		

Karen can't go between the 1st and the 8th of March.
Ruth can't go between the 25th and 31st of March.

Suggest a weekend when the sisters could go on holiday together.

1) First, cross out any dates when the sisters can't go.

2) Next, look for a weekend when both sisters are available.

(A weekend is Saturday to Sunday.)

March						
Sun	Mon	Tues	Wed	Thurs	Fri	Sat
		~~1~~	~~2~~	~~3~~	~~4~~	~~5~~
~~6~~	~~7~~	~~8~~	9	10	11	(12)
(13)	14	15	16	17	18	(19)
(20)	21	22	23	24	~~25~~	~~26~~
~~27~~	~~28~~	~~29~~	~~30~~	~~31~~		

So the sisters could go on holiday on the either the 12th-13th or 19th-20th. Pick one of these for your answer.

Practice Question

1) A town has a festival which starts on the second Sunday of May.

   a) On what date does the festival begin?

   ....

   b) The festival lasts for 7 days. On what date does it end?

   ....

MAY						
SUN	MON	TUES	WED	THURS	FRI	SAT
		1	2	3	4	5
6	7	8	9	10	11	12
13	14	15	16	17	18	19
20	21	22	23	24	25	26
27	28	29	30	31		

   c) On the 6th day of the festival there is a funfair. On what date does this happen?

   ....

Section Three — Dates and Time

Time

Time Has Lots of Different Units

You need to be able to use lots of different units for time. You also need to be able to change between them. Here are how some of the units of time are related:

60 seconds = 1 minute
60 minutes = 1 hour
24 hours = 1 day

7 days = 1 week
365 days = 1 year
12 months = 1 year

10 years = 1 decade
100 years = 1 century

15 minutes = a quarter of an hour
30 minutes = half an hour
45 minutes = three quarters of an hour

Examples

1) How many seconds are there in 2 minutes?

    There are 60 seconds in 1 minute, so to find out how many seconds there are in 2 minutes, you need to multiply 60 by 2:

    60 × 2 = **120 seconds**

2) How many days is 48 hours?

    1 day is the same as 24 hours, so to find out how many days there are in 48 hours, you need to divide 48 by 24:

    48 ÷ 24 = **2 days**

Practice Questions

1) How many minutes are there in half an hour? ....

2) How many days are there in a year? ....

3) How many days are there in 3 weeks?

    ....

The 12-Hour Clock and the 24-Hour Clock

1) You can give the time using the 12-hour clock or the 24-hour clock.

2) The 24-hour clock goes from 00:00 (midnight) to 23:59 (one minute before the next midnight).

   Example

   06:00 is 6 o'clock in the morning. 18:00 is 6 o'clock in the evening.

3) The 12-hour clock goes from 12:00 am (midnight) to 11:59 am (one minute before noon), and then from 12:00 pm (noon) till 11:59 pm (one minute before midnight).

   Example

   2:00 am is 2 o'clock in the morning. 2:00 pm is 2 o'clock in the afternoon.

   Noon is also called midday.

4) For times in the afternoon, you need to add 12 hours to go from the 12-hour clock to the 24-hour clock. Take away 12 hours to go from the 24-hour clock to the 12-hour clock.

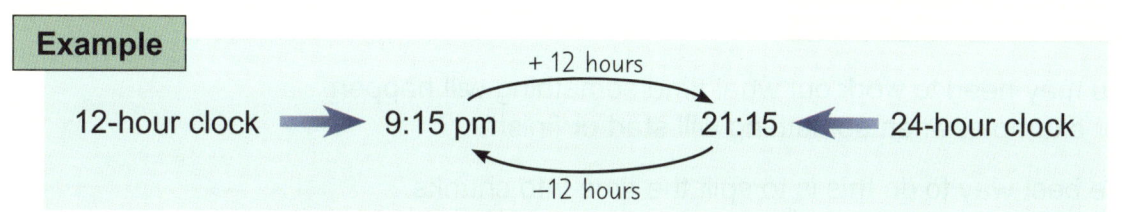

   Example

   12-hour clock → 9:15 pm + 12 hours → 21:15 ← 24-hour clock
                              −12 hours

Practice Questions

1) Change the times below from the 24-hour clock to the 12-hour clock.

   a) 10:30

   b) 15:35

2) Change the times below from the 12-hour clock to the 24-hour clock.

   a) 7:10 pm

   b) 5:20 am

3) Antony is meeting a friend at 9 pm. His watch reads 21:30 as he arrives. Is he late?

Section Three — Dates and Time

Working Out Lengths of Time

To work out how long something took, break it into parts.

Example

Kate set off on a bike ride at 10:30 am and had a break at 12:25 pm. How long had she been riding for?

10:30 am ⟶ 11:00 am ⟶ 12:00 pm ⟶ 12:25 pm
   30 mins   1 hour   25 mins

Add up the hours and minutes separately: 1 hour
30 mins + 25 mins = 55 mins

So she was riding for **1 hour and 55 mins**.

Working Out Times

1) You may need to work out what time something will happen. For example, when something will start or finish.

2) The best way to do this is to split the time into chunks.

Example 1

The time is 12:30 pm. Pete has a meeting in 45 minutes. What time does the meeting start?

12:30 pm ⟶ 1:00 pm ⟶ 1:15 pm
   30 mins   15 mins

Split the time before the meeting into two chunks.
30 mins + 15 mins = 45 mins.

Pete's meeting starts at **1:15 pm**.

Example 2

Dianne is going to watch a film at the cinema. The film lasts for 1 hour and 30 minutes. During the film there will be a 15 minute break.

If the film starts at 7:30 pm, what time will it finish?

7:30 pm ⟶ 8:30 pm ⟶ 9:00 pm ⟶ 9:15 pm
   1 hour   30 mins   15 mins
       Film time   Break

The film will finish at **9:15 pm**.

Section Three — Dates and Time

Practice Questions

1) A play starts at 7:00 pm and finishes at 9:30 pm. How long is the play?

   ....

   ....

2) Ryan catches a train at 10:55 am and gets off at 11:50 am. How long was his journey?

   ....

   ....

3) An electricity company are planning a power cut. They will switch the power off at 5:15 am and turn it back on at 9:30 am. How long will the power cut last?

   ....

   ....

4) Tom is expecting a phone call from his mother in three quarters of an hour. The time is now 18:45. What time will Tom's mother ring?

   ....

   ....

5) Kiera is going to a friend's house. Her journey involves a half hour bus ride and then a 10 minute walk. If she gets on the bus at 6:00 pm, what time will she arrive?

   ....

   ....

6) Gary sets off for the gym at 18:55. It takes him 20 minutes to walk there. If he stays at the gym until it closes at 21:00, how long will Gary have spent in the gym?

   ....

   ....

Section Three — Dates and Time

Timetables

Timetables Have Information About When Things Happen

1) Timetables have columns and rows.

2) Columns are the strips that go up and down. Rows are the strips that go across.

3) There are lots of different types of timetables — the best way to learn how to use them is to practise.

Example 1

The timetable below shows train times.
What time would you need to leave Preston to get to Deansgate for 12:30?

Preston	10:32	11:02	11:33	12:02
Buckshaw Parkway	10:44	11:14	11:45	12:14
Bolton	11:09	11:40	12:10	12:40
Deansgate	―	11:27	12:07	12:29	13:07

1) Find Deansgate in the timetable.

2) Follow that row until you reach the last time before 12:30. It's 12:29.

3) Go up the column till you reach the Preston row — this is the leaving time from Preston.

4) So you'd need to leave Preston at 11:33.

Example 2

The timetable for a country show is shown below.

	Saturday	Sunday
10:00 am	Livestock show	Bakery judging
11:00 am	Woodland walk	Tractor show
1:30 pm	Butchery class	Birds of prey show
2:30 pm	Lawnmower racing	Sheep shearing
3:00 pm	Brass band contest	Celebrity chefs

1) What time does the tractor show start?   Answer: 11:00 am (on Sunday).

2) On which day is the butchery class?   Answer: Saturday.

3) When is the birds of prey show?   Answer: 1:30 pm on Sunday.

You Need to be Able to Create Timetables

There are no set rules for making timetables. You just need to use the information you're given and put it together in a sensible way.

Example

Victoria is planning her son's birthday party.
The party will include:
- Party games
- Lunch
- A clown show

Draw a timetable for the party. Think about how long each activity will last and what time the party will start and finish.

Answer:

There isn't just one right answer for this question. There are lots of timetables that would work. Here's what you might do:

1) Pick a start time for the party. It's a children's party, so let's say 11 am.

2) Decide a sensible order for the activities to go in.
   For example, you'd probably wouldn't start off with lunch.

3) Think about how long each activity might last.
   - For example, party games might last for 1 hour.
   - Lunch might last for 1 hour.
   - The clown show might last for 30 minutes.

4) Then work out what time each activity will start and finish.

Your timetable might end up looking something like this:

	Start	Finish
Party games	11 am	12 pm
Lunch	12 pm	1 pm
Clown show	1 pm	1.30 pm

Make sure none of the activities overlap.

Section Three — Dates and Time

Practice Questions

1) Debbie wants to travel by train from St David's to Topsham.

   a) If she wants to get there by 17:30, which train should she catch?

St David's	16:25	16:55	17:25
St James Park	16:29	17:01	17:29
Digby	16:33	17:07	17:33
Topsham	16:39	17:13	17:39

   ....

   b) She now needs to be there by 17:15 instead. Can she catch the same train from St David's?

   ....

2) Lynn is going on a one day training course. Her timetable for the day is shown below.

   a) What time does 'Reptile Care' start?

   ....

Time	Activity
09:00 - 10:45	Introduction
10:45 - 11:00	Morning Break
11:00 - 12:45	Large Animal Care
12:45 - 13:30	Lunch
13:30 - 15:00	Reptile Care
15:00 - 15:30	Afternoon Break
15:30 - 17:00	Marine Animal Care

   b) How long is 'Large Animal Care'?

   ....

   c) Which is longer — morning break or afternoon break?

   ....

3) Taneeka is organising a fashion show. The show will start at 7:30 pm.
   There will be:
   - A catwalk lasting 1 hour.
   - A party with food and drink.

   Write a timetable for the show. You'll need to allow time for guests to arrive and sit down at the start. You should also choose a sensible time for the show to finish.

Section Three — Dates and Time

Section Four — Shape and Space

Angles

Angles Tell You the Size of a Corner

1) This is an angle.

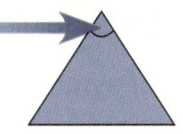

2) Angles can be big or small.

3) Smaller angles are sharp and pointy. Bigger angles are wide and flat.

Examples

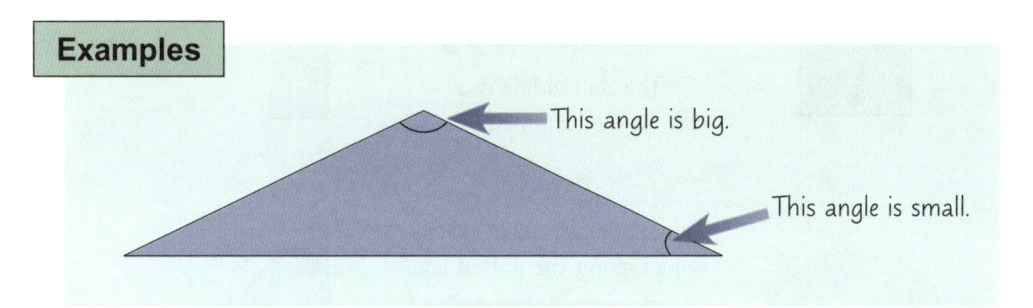

This angle is big.

This angle is small.

4) A right angle is a special type of angle. A right angle looks like this:

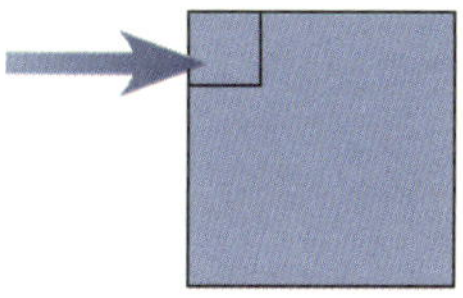

5) To spot a right angle, look for a square corner.

Practice Questions

1) Which angle is bigger, A or B?

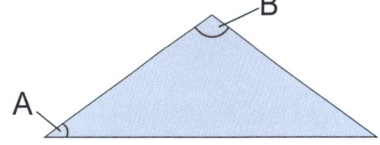

   ....

2) Write down the number of right angles in the following shapes.

   a)    b)   c)

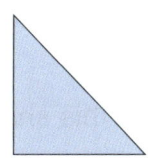

   ....

Section Four — Shape and Space

Lines of Symmetry

Some Shapes Have a Line of Symmetry

1) You can find out whether a shape has a line of symmetry by folding it in half.

2) If the sides fold together exactly, then the fold is a line of symmetry.

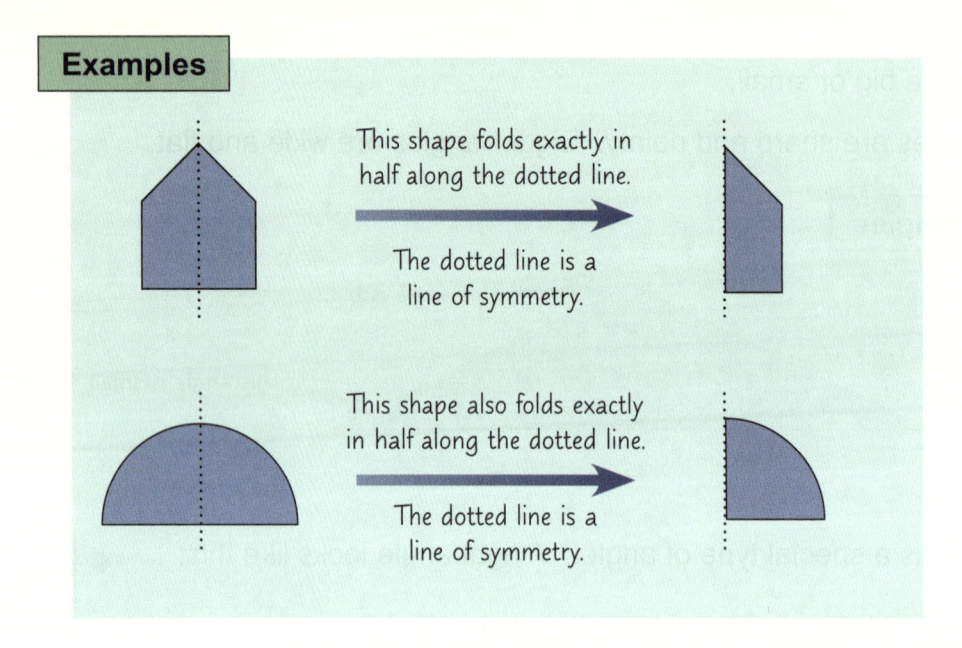

Examples

This shape folds exactly in half along the dotted line.

The dotted line is a line of symmetry.

This shape also folds exactly in half along the dotted line.

The dotted line is a line of symmetry.

Some Shapes Have More Than One Line of Symmetry

Some shapes have two or more lines of symmetry.

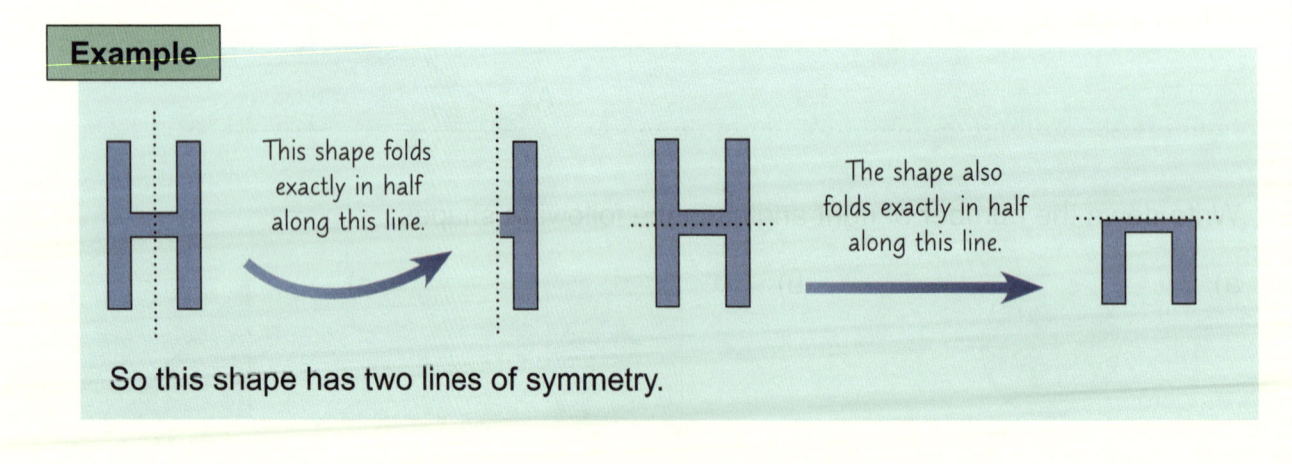

Example

This shape folds exactly in half along this line.

The shape also folds exactly in half along this line.

So this shape has two lines of symmetry.

Lines of symmetry can go up and down, left to right or corner to corner.

Section Four — Shape and Space

Some Shapes Have No Lines of Symmetry

Some shapes won't fold exactly in half, no matter where you fold them.

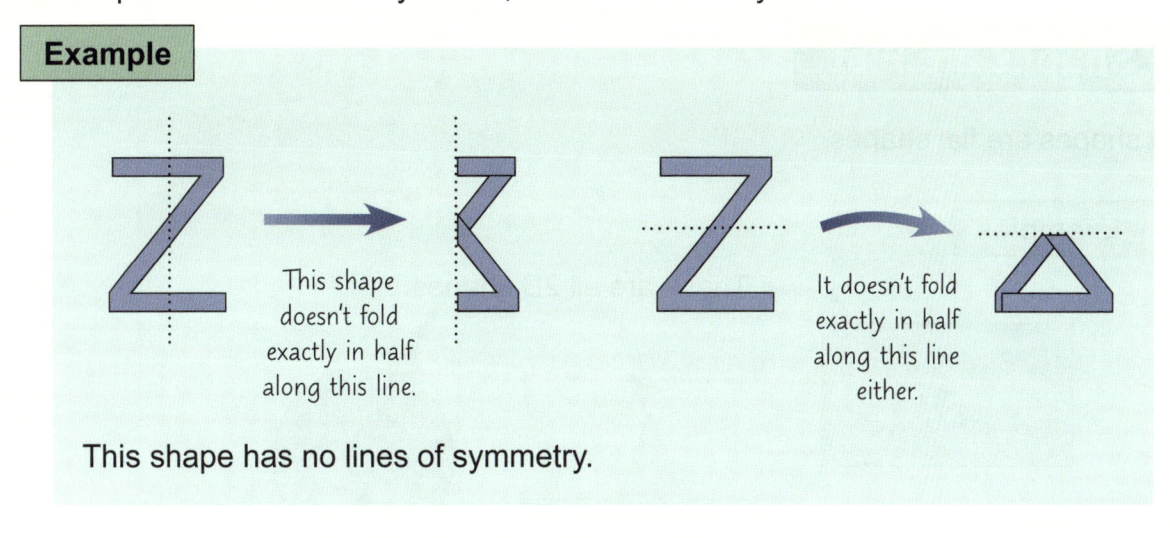

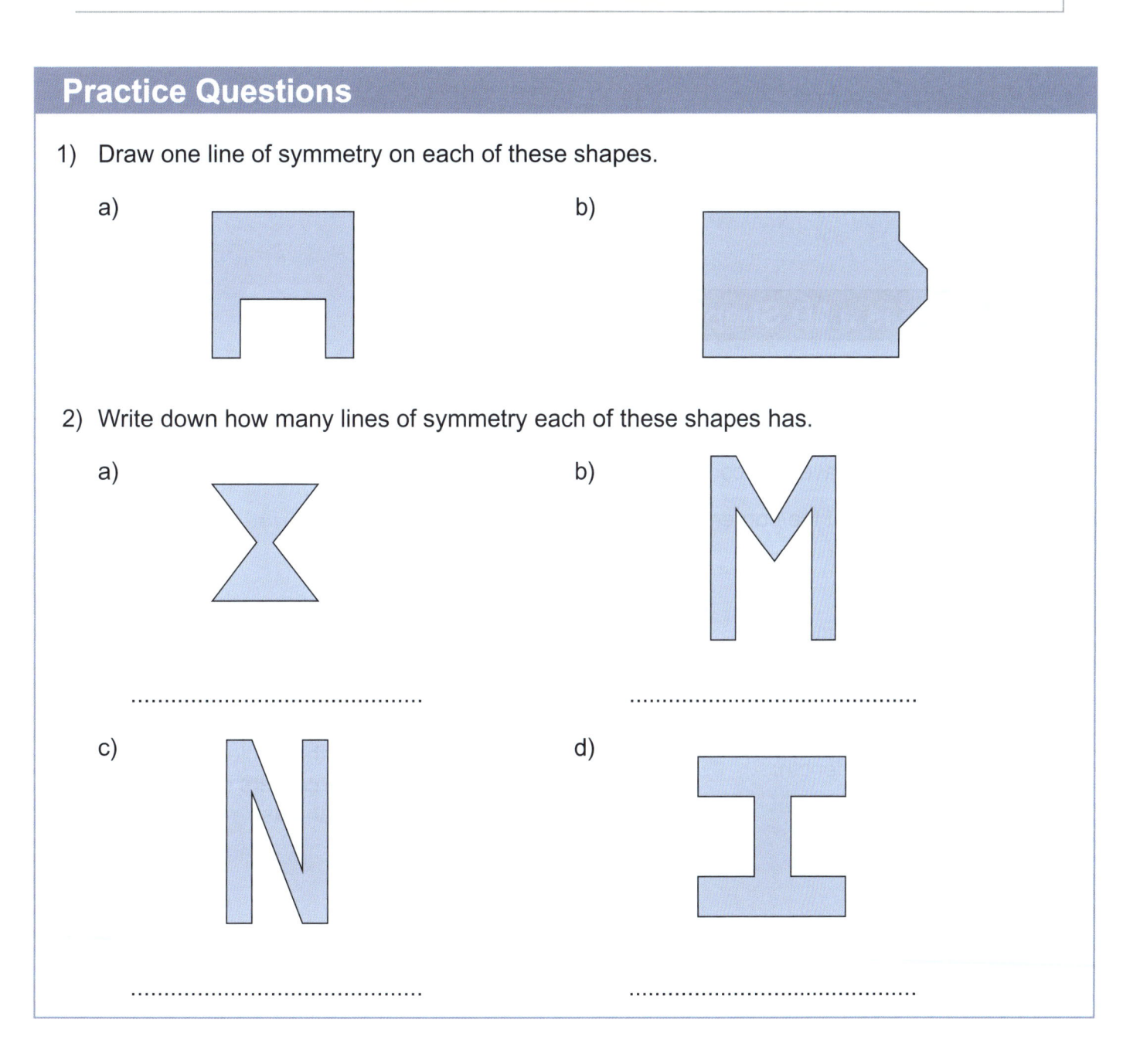

Example

This shape doesn't fold exactly in half along this line.

It doesn't fold exactly in half along this line either.

This shape has no lines of symmetry.

Practice Questions

1) Draw one line of symmetry on each of these shapes.

   a)

   b)

2) Write down how many lines of symmetry each of these shapes has.

   a)

   b)

   ....

   c)

   d)

   ....

Section Four — Shape and Space

2D Shapes

2D Shapes are Flat

2D shapes are flat shapes.

Examples

These are all 2D shapes.

A Square is a 2D Shape

1) Squares have four straight sides.
2) All the sides are the same length.
3) Squares also have four corners.
4) All the angles at the corners are right angles.   A right angle is a square corner.

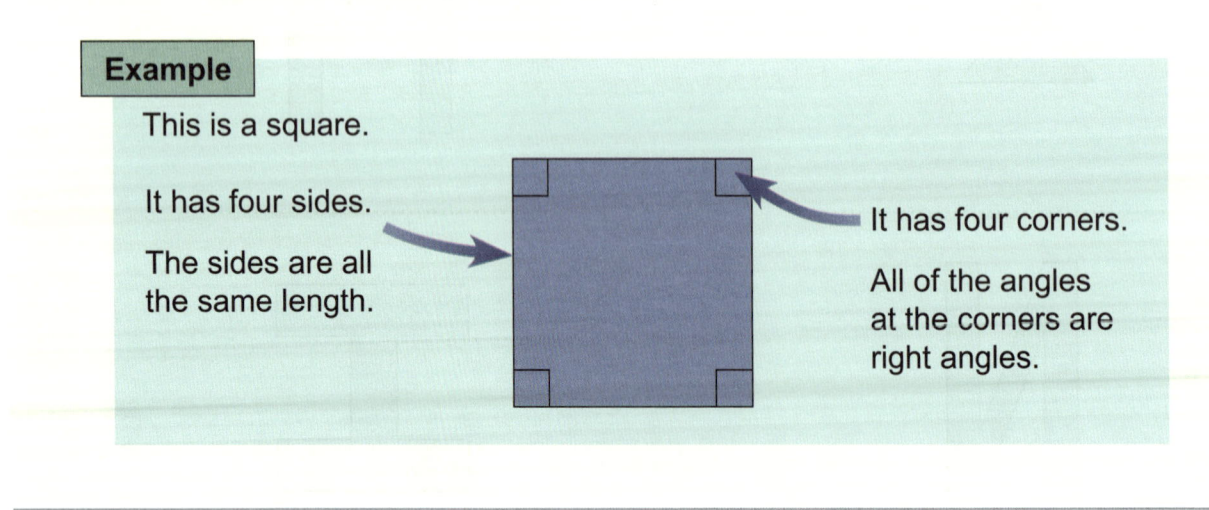

Example

This is a square.

It has four sides.

The sides are all the same length.

It has four corners.

All of the angles at the corners are right angles.

Section Four — Shape and Space

Rectangles are 2D Shapes

1) Rectangles have four straight sides.
2) Sides that are opposite each other are the same length.
3) Rectangles also have four corners.
4) All the angles at the corners are right angles.

Example

This is a rectangle.

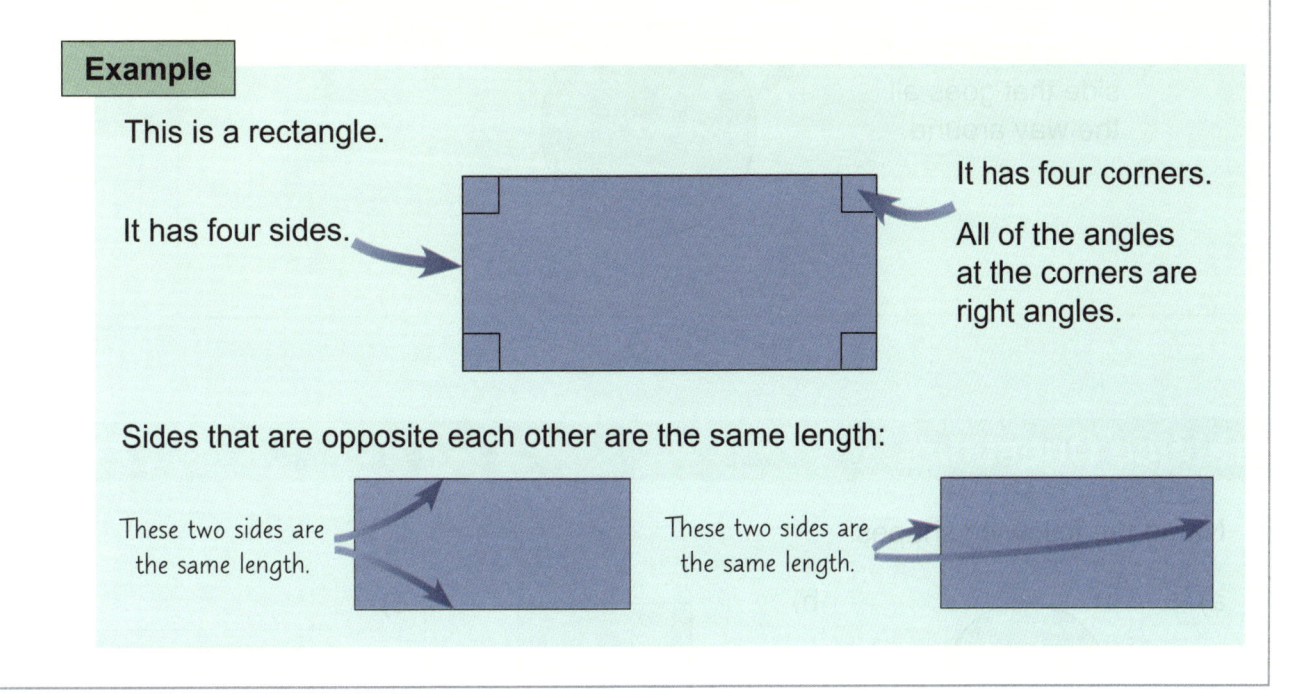

It has four sides.

It has four corners.

All of the angles at the corners are right angles.

Sides that are opposite each other are the same length:

These two sides are the same length.

These two sides are the same length.

Triangles are 2D Shapes

1) Triangles have three straight sides. The sides can be different lengths.
2) Triangles also have three corners. The angles at the corners can be different sizes.

Example

This is a triangle.

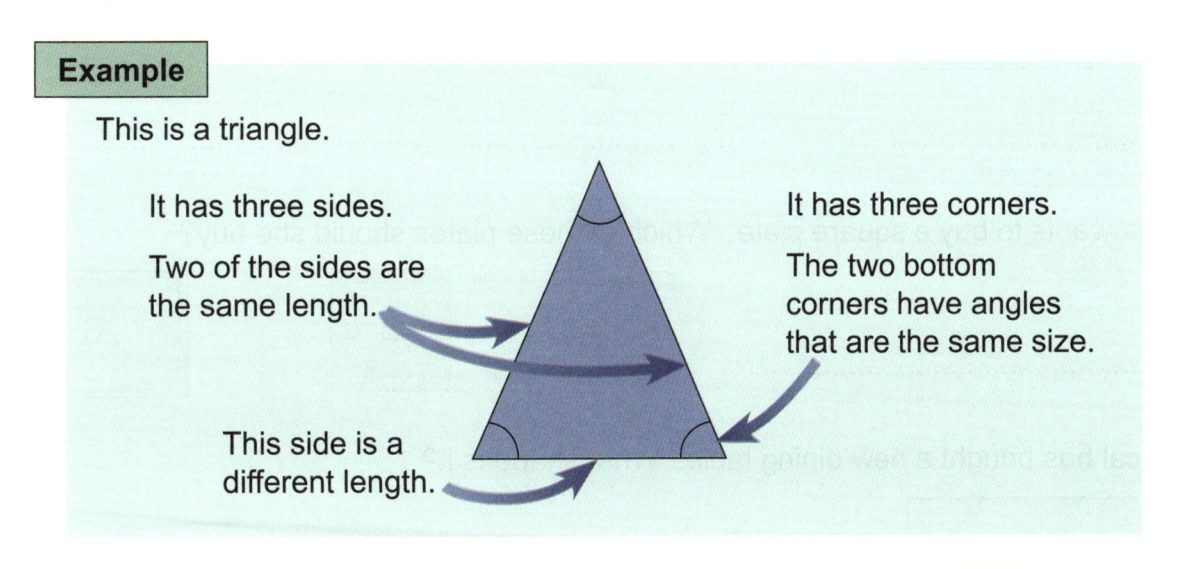

It has three sides.

Two of the sides are the same length.

It has three corners.

The two bottom corners have angles that are the same size.

This side is a different length.

Section Four — Shape and Space

Circles are 2D Shapes

1) Circles have one curved side.
2) They don't have any corners.

Example

This is a circle.

It has one curved side that goes all the way around.

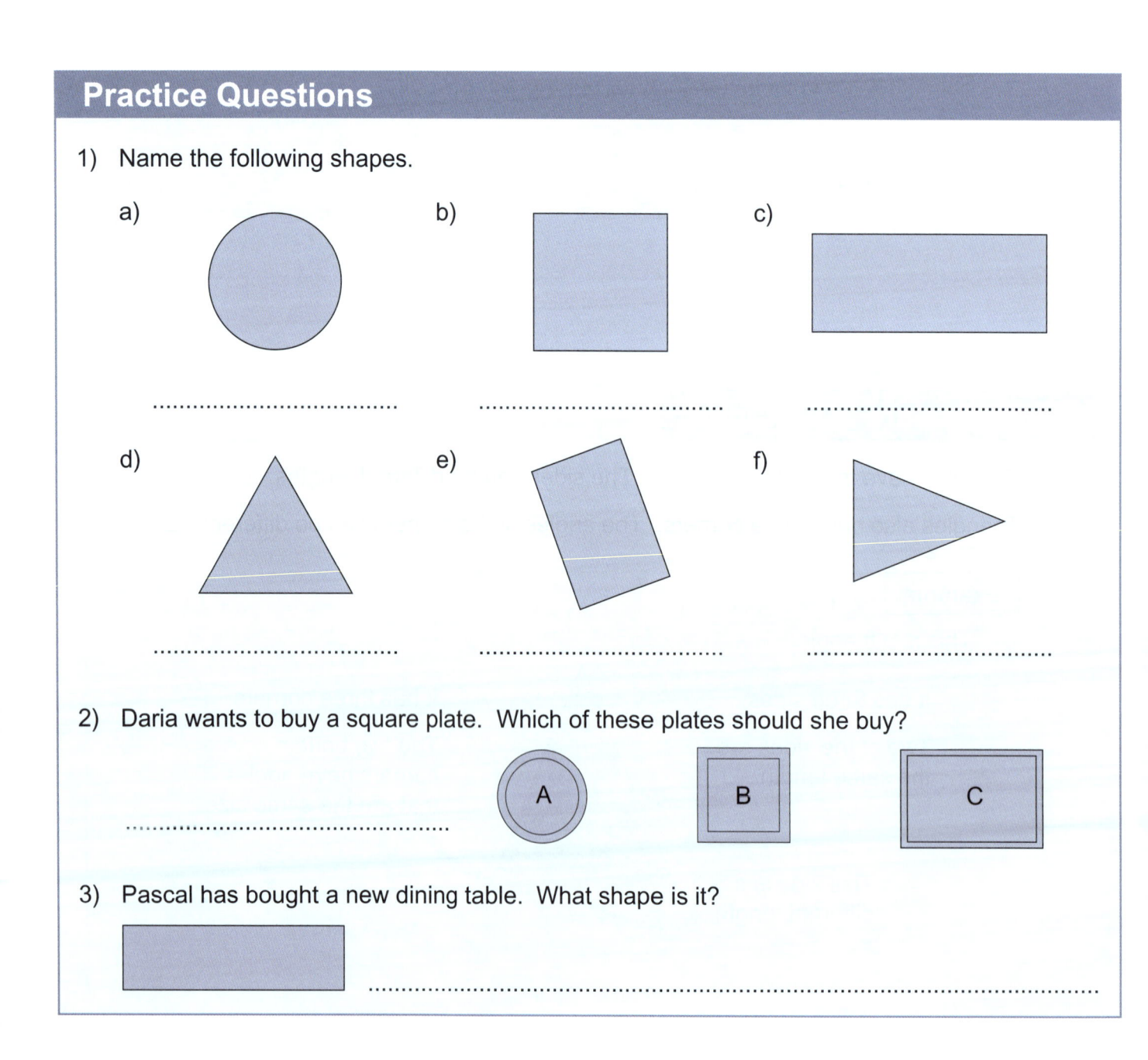

It has no corners.

Practice Questions

1) Name the following shapes.

   a)

   b)

   c)

   ....

   d)

   e)

   f)

   ....

2) Daria wants to buy a square plate. Which of these plates should she buy?

   A   B   C

   ....

3) Pascal has bought a new dining table. What shape is it?

   ....

Section Four — Shape and Space

3D Shapes

3D Shapes are Solid

3D shapes are solid shapes.

You need to know these 3D shapes...

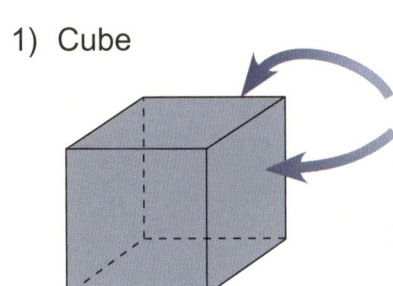

1) Cube

   1) All the flat parts of a cube are squares.
   2) A cube has lots of corners.
   3) All the angles at the corners are right angles.

2) Cuboid

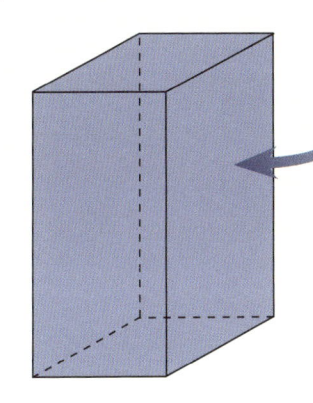

   1) Some of the flat parts of a cuboid are rectangles.
   2) A cuboid has lots of corners.
   3) All the angles at the corners are right angles.

3) Cylinder

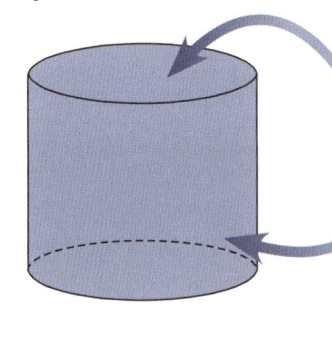

   1) The flat parts of a cylinder are circles.
   2) A cylinder has no corners.
   3) It has one curved side.

Section Four — Shape and Space

Practice Questions

1) Name the following shapes.

    a)   b)   c)

    ....

2) Look at the sofa cushion on the right.
   What shape is it?

   ....

3) Tracy wants a new coffee table. She wants it to be a cylinder.
   Which solid should she choose — A, B or C?

   A   B   C

   ....

4) Anthony is using some modelling bricks.
   What two 3D shapes is this brick made up of?

   A .... and a ....

Section Four — Shape and Space

Plans

Plans Show How Things are Laid Out in an Area

1) A plan shows the layout of an area. For example, a plan might show a room and all the objects in it.

2) Plans are drawn as if you are looking down on the area from above.

3) Plans show objects as 2D shapes. For example as squares or rectangles.

Example

A plan of a room is shown below:

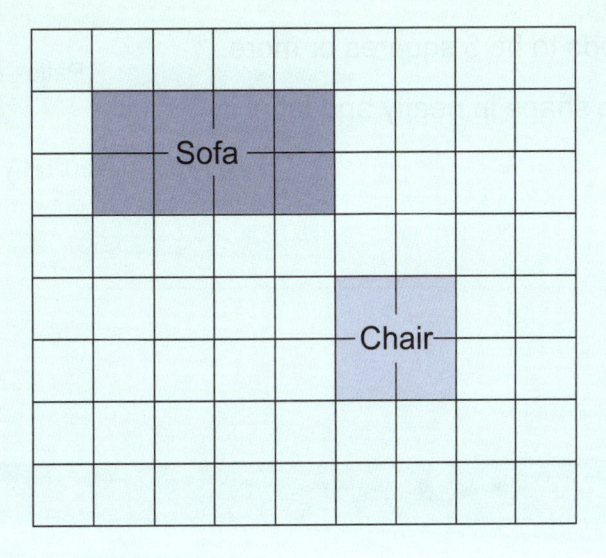

The plan has been drawn on a grid.

The squares in the grid are all the same size.

You can tell how big each object is by counting how many squares it covers.

The sofa is 4 squares long. The chair is 2 squares long.

4 ÷ 2 = 2

So the sofa is twice (2 times) as long as the chair.

Another way to say this is that the chair is half as long as the sofa.

Section Four — Shape and Space

Using Plans

Plans are useful for deciding where a new object will fit in an area.

Example

A plan of a garden is shown on the right.

Draw a patio on the plan. It must be a rectangle. It must be bigger than the shed.

1) Think about the shape you need to draw. A rectangle has 4 sides and the sides opposite each other are the same length.

2) Work out what size the shape needs to be. It must be bigger than the shed, which is 4 squares.
So it needs to be 5 squares or more.

3) Draw the shape in neatly and label it.

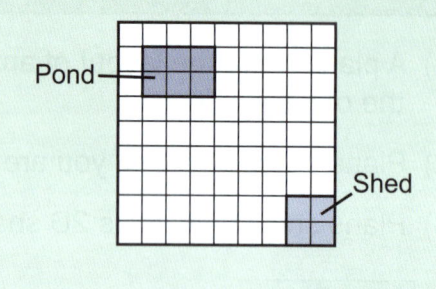

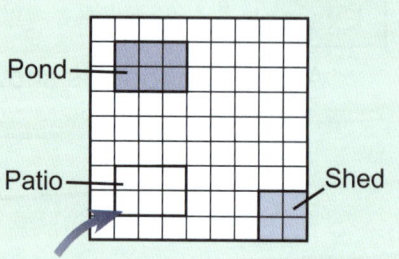

The question doesn't tell you where to put the patio, so you can draw it in any empty space.

Practice Questions

1) Sharon is designing her new kitchen. A plan of it is shown on the right.

   a) What shape is the table?

   ....

   b) The fridge is the same size as the cooker. Draw a square to show where the fridge could go.

2) A plan of Sarah's room is shown on the right.

   Sarah wants to put a set of drawers next to her bed.
   - The drawers are twice as big as the TV.
   - They are square.

   Draw the set of drawers on the plan.

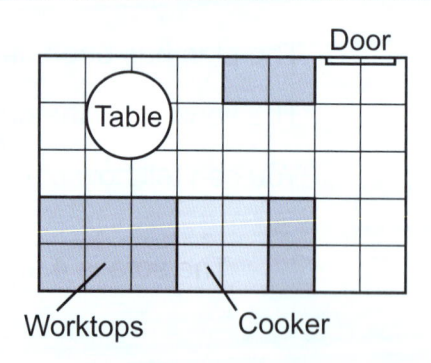

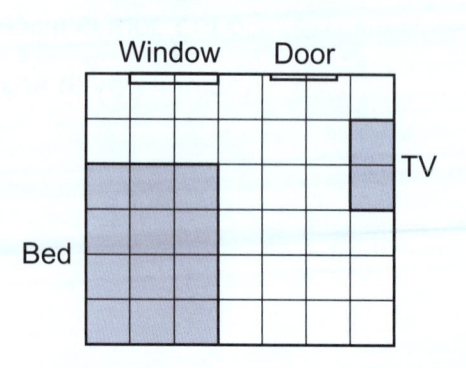

Section Four — Shape and Space

Movement and Direction

Describing Movement

Movement can be described by talking about direction.

1) **Clockwise** — movement in the same direction as the hands of a clock.

2) **Anticlockwise** — movement in the opposite direction to the hands of a clock.

3) **Left** — movement towards the left.

4) **Right** — movement towards the right.

You can also talk about the amount of movement.

1) **Whole turn** — turning one whole circle.

2) **Half turn** — turning half a circle.

3) **Quarter turn** — turning a quarter of a circle.

Example

The dial on an oven is set to 0°.
The dial is turned half a turn to the right.

What temperature is the oven set to now?

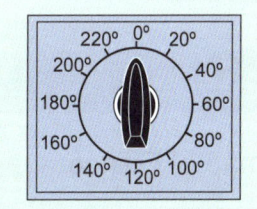

1) Half a turn means turning half a circle.

2) To the right is going this way:

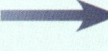

3) So the dial moves like this:

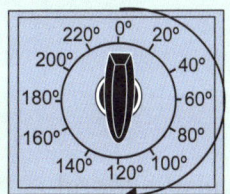

The oven is set to **120°**.

Section Four — Shape and Space

The Four Compass Points

1) The four compass points are North, South, East and West.

2) Starting at North and going clockwise, the compass points always follow the same order. Use this rhyme to help you remember the order:

Never (North), Eat (East), Soggy (South), Wheat (West).

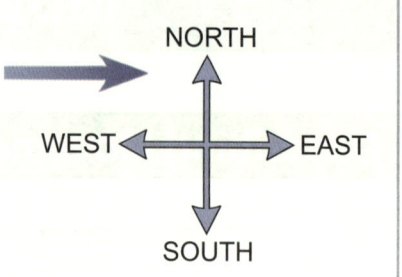

3) You can use compass points to give directions.

Example

Bailey is going to Bolton. She's travelling north on the M56. When she joins the M60, should she go east or west?

1) She's travelling north (up the page) on the M56. When she joins the M60 she needs to go to the left, towards the M61 and Bolton.

2) To work out whether left is east or west, fill in the missing compass points:

Never (North), Eat (East), Soggy (South), Wheat (West).

The compass should look like this:

So left is west.

'N' on a compass means 'North'. 'E' means 'East', 'S' means 'South' and 'W' means 'West'.

3) She should join the M60 going **west**.

Practice Question

1) Look at the map of France.

   a) Is Paris east or west of Alençon?

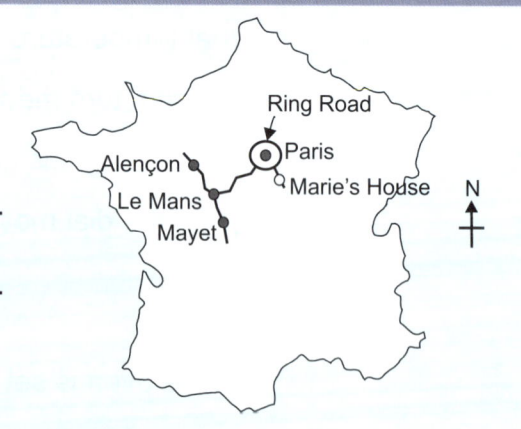

   ....

   ....

   Marie lives south of Paris.
   She is driving to Mayet to visit a friend.

   b) Should she go clockwise or anticlockwise along the Paris ring road?

   ....

   c) Which direction should she head in from Le Mans?

   ....

Section Four — Shape and Space

Section Five — Handling Data

Lists

Lists Can Be Used to Show Information

1) A list is a simple way of showing information.

2) Another word for information is data.

3) The data in a list can be in words, numbers or both.

Examples

1) A shopping list: ➡ Bread, Milk, Tea, Biscuits

   This shows what you need to buy from the shops.

2) A price list for a hairdressers: ➡

Wash and blow dry	£15
Cut and blow dry	£20
Cut and colour	£35

   This shows how much different services cost at a hairdressers.

Using the Information in Lists

You need to be able to use information from lists.

Example 1

This is the price list for a furniture store:

large bookcase	£50
small bookcase	£45
desk	£40
delivery charge	£10

How much will it cost to buy the small bookcase and get it delivered?

Answer:

1) Read down the list until you find the small bookcase. Then read across to find the price: £45

2) Read down the list until you find the word 'delivery'. Read across to find the price: £10

3) Now add the two prices together: £45 + £10 = £55

   So it will cost **£55** to buy the small bookcase and get it delivered.

Section Five — Handling Data

> **Example 2**
>
> Karen, Hannah and Jo are arranging to meet up.
> Jo makes a list of the dates when each of them is free.
>
> Jo: 10th, 12th 20th
> Karen: 9th, 12th, 16th
> Hannah: 6th, 9th, 12th
>
> What date are all three friends free to meet up?
>
> Answer: look for a date that appears after each girl's name.
>
> 1) Start at the beginning of the list. The first date Jo is free is the 10th.
>
> 2) Now look at the dates after Karen's name. Karen is not free on the 10th. So the girls can't meet up on the 10th.
>
> 3) The next date Jo is free is the 12th.
>
> 4) Check the dates after Karen's name again. Karen is also free on the 12th.
>
> 5) Now check the dates after Hannah's name. Hannah is free on the 12th.
>
> So all three friends are free to meet up on the 12th.

Practice Questions

1) The list below shows how much weight each person in a weight loss group has lost.

   a) How much weight has Faye lost?

   ....

   b) Who has lost the most weight?

   ....

Tina	0.45 kg
Faye	0.9 kg
Danni	0.4 kg
Thom	1.35 kg

2) Look at the menu on the right.

   a) How much will it cost to buy soup and a sandwich?

   ....

   b) How much more expensive is the tea cake than the scone?

   ....

Tea cake	£1.10
Soup	£1.20
Sandwich	£1.60
Scone	£1.00

Section Five — Handling Data

Tables

Tables are a Way of Showing Information

Tables show information in columns and rows.

They're often easier to read than lists.

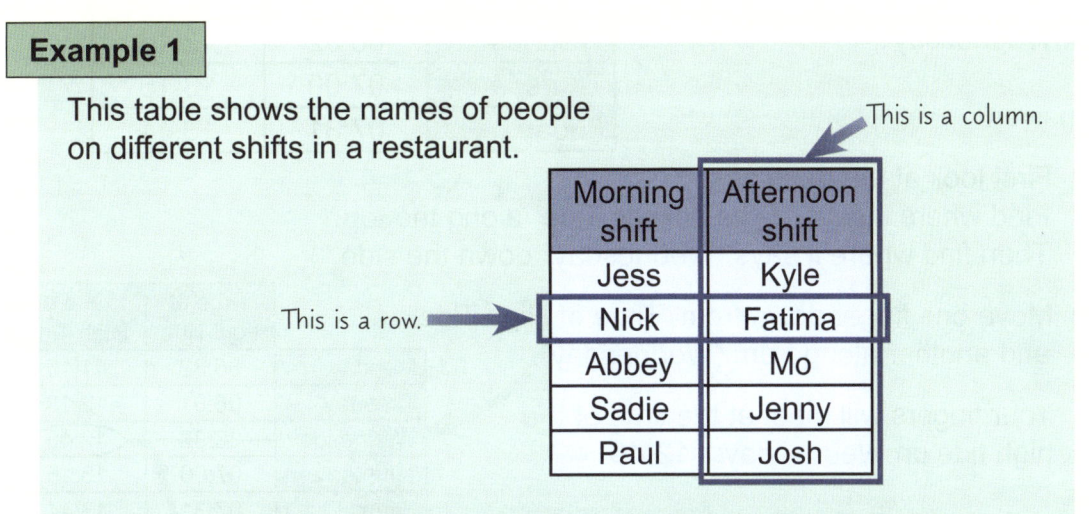

Example 1

This table shows the names of people on different shifts in a restaurant.

This is a column.

This is a row.

Morning shift	Afternoon shift
Jess	Kyle
Nick	Fatima
Abbey	Mo
Sadie	Jenny
Paul	Josh

It shows that Jess, Nick, Abbey, Sadie and Paul are on the morning shift, and Kyle, Fatima, Mo, Jenny and Josh are on the afternoon shift.

Example 2

This table gives you information about two different people — Tim and Steph.

	Tim	Steph
Favourite food	Pizza	Pasta
Favourite drink	Coffee	Tea
Favourite sport	Squash	Tennis
Favourite hobby	Chess	Singing

The words in the dark blue boxes are headings. They tell you what's in the rest of the table.

For example, it tells you that Tim's favourite sport is squash and Steph's favourite sport is tennis.

Section Five — Handling Data

Using the Information in Tables

You need to be able to use information in tables.

Example 1

The table shows the times of the low and high tides at a beach.

What is the time of the high tide on Wednesday?

	Time of Low Tide	Time of High Tide
Monday	05:32	11:45
Tuesday	06:01	12:13
Wednesday	06:32	12:46
Thursday	07:00	13:15
Friday	07:31	13:44

Answer:

1) First look at the headings.
   Find where it says "Time of High Tide" along the top.
   Then find where it says "Wednesday" down the side.

2) Move one finger down from "Time of High Tide" and another along from "Wednesday".

   Your fingers will meet at the time of the high tide on Wednesday: **12:46**.

You can draw lines to help you if you like.

Example 2

A group of people were asked if they were left-handed or right-handed. The results are shown in the table below.

	Women	Men
Left-handed	36	27
Right-handed	164	173

How many women took part in the survey?

Answer: add up the number of left-handed women and the number of right-handed women.

36 + 164 = **200**

How many people were right-handed?

Answer: add up the number of right-handed women and the number of right-handed men.

164 + 173 = **337**

Section Five — Handling Data

Practice Questions

1) The table on the right shows the times of sunrise and sunset during a week.

	Time of Sunrise	Time of Sunset
Monday	07:01	19:08
Tuesday	07:03	19:07
Wednesday	07:04	19:05
Thursday	07:05	19:03
Friday	07:07	19:01

   a) What time is sunrise on Tuesday?

   ....

   b) What time is sunset on Friday?

   ....

   c) Is sunset later on Wednesday or on Thursday?

   ....

2) A survey was done to find out people's favourite type of film. The results of the survey are shown in the table.

	Women	Men
Romance	57	43
Horror	20	40
Sci-fi	32	35
Action	66	57

   a) How many men liked Horror films best?

   ....

   b) How many women took part in the survey?

   ....

   ....

   c) How many people said that Action films were their favourite type of film?

   ....

3) Claire wants to buy a wedding present for her friend. Part of her friend's wedding list is shown in the table below.

	Price	Already bought
Wine glasses	£60	
Candles	£36	✔
Lamp shade	£40	
Salad bowl	£45	
Silver photo frame	£55	✔

The presents are quite expensive.
Some of them have already been bought by other people.

Claire wants to buy her friend the cheapest present she can, that hasn't already been bought. Which present should she choose?

....

Section Five — Handling Data

Charts and Graphs

Tally Charts Help You Record What You've Counted

Tally charts are good if you need to count something.
For example, the number of different types of bird in a park.

Example

1) Each line in the chart is called a tally mark.

2) In this case, 1 tally mark means 1 bird has been seen.

3) To find out how many of each bird has been seen, count up the tally marks.

Type of bird	Tally
Robin	II
Blue tit	III
Sparrow	I
Pigeon	III
Seagull	ⅲ̄̄ I

There are 2 robins.
There are 3 blue tits.
There is 1 sparrow.
There are 3 pigeons.
There are 6 seagulls.

In a tally, every 5th mark crosses a group of 4 like this: ⅲ̄̄
So ⅲ̄̄ I means 6 (a group of 5 plus 1).

Practice Question

1) A travel agent does a survey to find out what people's favourite type of holiday is. The travel agent collects people's answers in a tally chart.

Favourite type of holiday	Tally
Beach	IIII
Skiing	
Safari	ⅲ̄̄ II
Cruise	ⅲ̄̄ ⅲ̄̄
Sightseeing	ⅲ̄̄ I

a) How many people said that a beach holiday was their favourite type of holiday?

....

b) How many people said a cruise was their favourite type of holiday?

....

c) Six people said that their favourite type of holiday was skiing.
Fill this in on the tally chart.

Section Five — Handling Data

Bar Charts Let You Compare Data

1) A bar chart is a simple way of showing data (information).

2) Data is shown on a bar chart as bars.

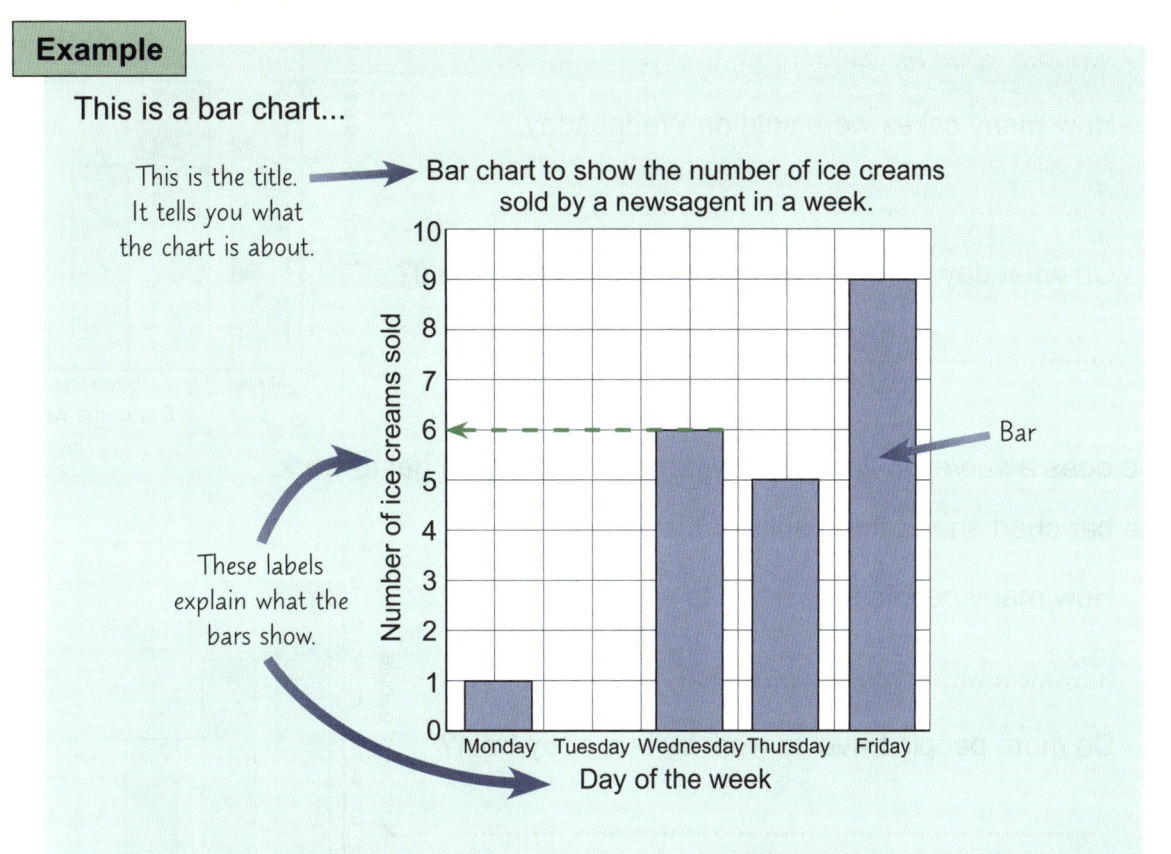

Example

This is a bar chart...

This is the title. It tells you what the chart is about. → Bar chart to show the number of ice creams sold by a newsagent in a week.

These labels explain what the bars show.

← Bar

(Y-axis: Number of ice creams sold, 0 to 10)
(X-axis: Day of the week — Monday, Tuesday, Wednesday, Thursday, Friday)

Monday: 1, Tuesday: 0, Wednesday: 6, Thursday: 5, Friday: 9

1) The height of each bar shows how many ice creams were sold each day.

2) Just read across from the top of the bar to the number at the side.
   (You can draw a line if it helps.)

   For example, on Wednesday, 6 ice creams were sold.

3) The tallest bar is on Friday.
   This means that the most ice creams were sold on Friday.

4) There is no bar on Tuesday.
   This means that no ice creams were sold on Tuesday.

Section Five — Handling Data

Practice Questions

1) The bar chart shows the number of cakes sold in a bakery each day.

   a) How many cakes were sold on Monday?

   ....

   b) How many cakes were sold on Wednesday?

   ....

   c) On what day were the fewest number of cakes sold?

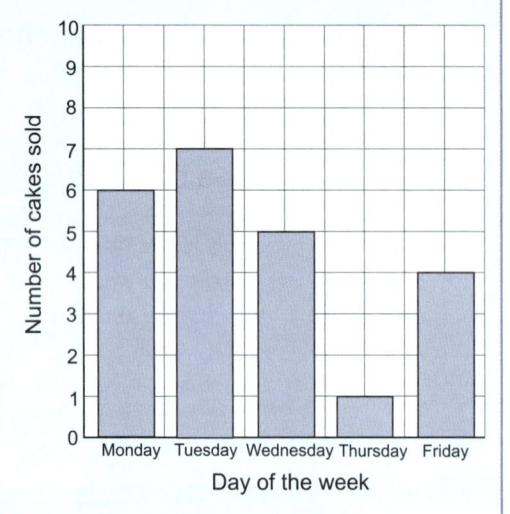

   ....

2) Lisa does a survey to find out how people in her office get to work.

   The bar chart shows the results of Lisa's survey.

   a) How many people take a taxi to work?

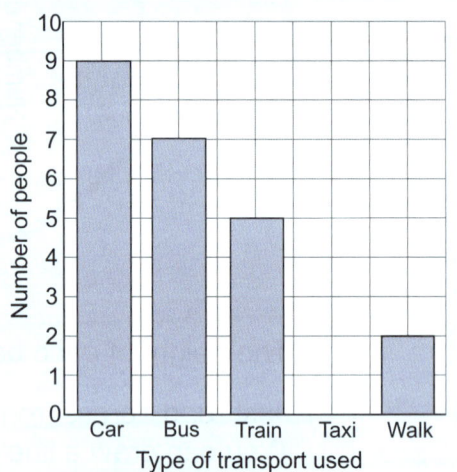

   ....

   b) Do more people travel to work by bus or by train?

   ....

   c) What is the most common way for people to get to work?

   ....

   Lisa forgot to include the number of people who ride a bike to work on the bar chart.

   d) 3 people ride a bike to work.

   How many more people ride a bike than walk?

   ....

   ....

Section Five — Handling Data

Line Graphs Can Show How Things Change Over Time

1) Line graphs are useful for showing things that change over time. For example, distance or temperature.

2) Data is shown on a line graph as a line.

Example

A firework is launched into the air. The line graph below shows how the height of the firework changes over time.

1) Each cross is a piece of data.

   For example, the cross at 2 seconds shows that the firework is **40 metres** high after **2 seconds**.

   The cross at 5 seconds shows that the firework is halfway between 20 metres and 30 metres high after **5 seconds**. This means it is **25 metres** high.

   25 is halfway between 20 and 30.

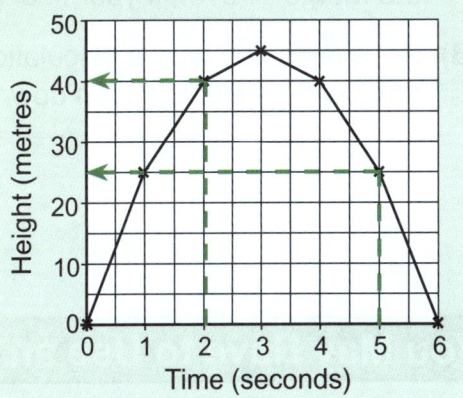

2) You can use the graph to find out the height of the firework at any time up to 6 seconds. For example, to find the height of the firework at 4.5 seconds...

   - Draw a line up to the graph from 4.5 seconds. (Halfway between 4 and 5.)
   - Then draw a line across to find out the height. It's between 30 and 35 metres high — probably about **33 metres**.

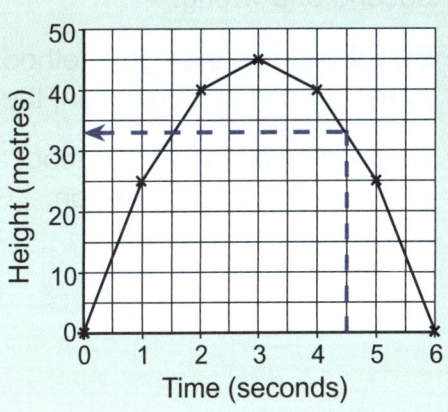

Practice Question

1) The line graph shows how the temperature in a garden changed during the morning.

   a) What was the temperature at 8.00?

   ....

   b) What was the temperature at 9.30?

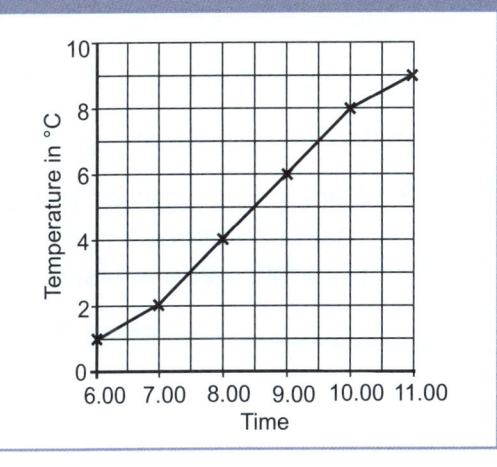

   ....

Test Help

Always Show Your Working

1) In the test it's really important that you show all of your working — there are lots of marks for the methods you use and the calculations that you do.

2) If you don't show how you worked your answer out, you may not get all of the marks — even if your final answer is right.

3) So, even if you type a calculation into your calculator to work it out, you must write the calculation down for the examiner to see as well.

You May Have to Use an Answer in Another Calculation

1) Sometimes you may need to use the answer to one question to work out the answer to another question.

2) If you get the answer to the first question wrong, you'll also get the answer to the second one wrong.

3) BUT if you use the right method, and you use the answer that you got for the first question in your calculation, then you can still get full marks for the second question.

4) So even if you're unsure about an answer, don't give up — make sure you keep going until the end of the question.

Always Check Your Answers

It's really important that you check your answers. Checking your answers helps you to spot mistakes that you've made, and in some questions there are marks for showing that you've checked your answer. There are lots of ways you can check answers. For example...

1) Reverse the calculation (see pages 7 and 12 for more on this).

2) Do the calculation again using a different method to see if you get the same answer.

3) Think about whether your answer is sensible. For example, if you're working out the cost of someone's lunch and your answer comes out as hundreds of pounds then you've probably made a mistake somewhere.

Task 1 — An Evening Out

1. (a) Wayne and Monica are going to the theatre to watch a play.

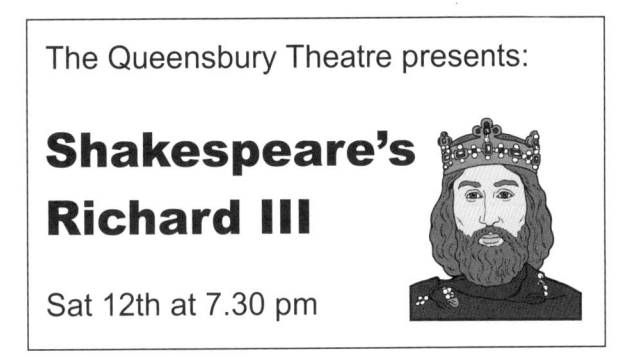

The Queensbury Theatre presents:

Shakespeare's Richard III

Sat 12th at 7.30 pm

Bus timetable:

Churchton	1605	1705	1805	1905
Bishops Mill	1635	1735	1835	1935
Farthing Street	1650	1750	1850	1950
The High School	1655	1755	1855	1955
The Queensbury Theatre	1700	1800	1900	2000
Station Road	1715	1815	1915	2015

(i) What time does the play start in the 24-hour clock?

....
(1 mark)

Wayne and Monica live in Bishops Mill. They need to get to the theatre at least 15 minutes before the play starts.

(ii) What time should they catch the bus?

....
(1 mark)

Test-style Questions

(b) Wayne and Monica are both students.

Queensbury Theatre

What's on: *Richard III*

Prices for tonight's show:

	Circle	Stalls
Adult	£30	£35
OAP	£25	£28
Student	£25	£28
Child (under 16)	£15	£17

(i) How much would it cost them to buy two student tickets in the circle?

....

....

(1 mark)

(ii) How much more expensive would it be for them both to sit in the stalls?

....

....

....

(2 marks)

Test-style Questions

(c) At the interval, Wayne and Monica buy some ice creams.

Ice cream

Single-scoop £1.50 Double-scoop £2.50

Buy two double-scoop ice creams and only pay half the price

They buy two double-scoop ice creams.

(i) How much should they pay without the special offer?

....
(1 mark)

(ii) How much do they pay with the special offer?

....

....
(1 mark)

(d) Wayne and Monica decide to get a taxi home. They live 10 miles from the theatre. The taxi charges £1.25 per mile.

(i) How much does it cost them to get home?

....
(1 mark)

(ii) Show how you check your calculation.

....
(1 mark)

Test-style Questions

Task 2 — Hosting a Dinner Party

2. Arthur is hosting a dinner party.
He has invited Susie, Neil, Duncan, Tyson and Sarah.

Tasty Treats

5 per box

Serve hot
Cook for 15 min
at 200°C or
at gas mark 6

(a) (i) Arthur would like each person to have 3 Tasty Treats with a drink before dinner.
How many packs of Tasty Treats should he buy?

....

....

....

....

....

....
(5 marks)

(ii) Arthur's guests will be arriving at 7.15 pm.
He'd like to serve the Tasty Treats half an hour later.
What time should he put them in the oven?

....

....

....
(2 marks)

(b) Arthur decides to make Yorkshire puddings as a starter.

Yorkshire puddings
(makes 3 large ones)
70 g plain flour
2 eggs
100 ml milk
mustard (to taste)

Flour

(i) How much flour does Arthur need to make 6 Yorkshire puddings?

....

....
(2 marks)

(ii) Arthur has added some flour to the scales.
How much more flour does Arthur need to weigh out?
Show how you check your calculation.

....

....

....
(3 marks)

Test-style Questions

(c) Arthur has bought a new table cloth on the Internet.
The table cloth is 2.55 m long.

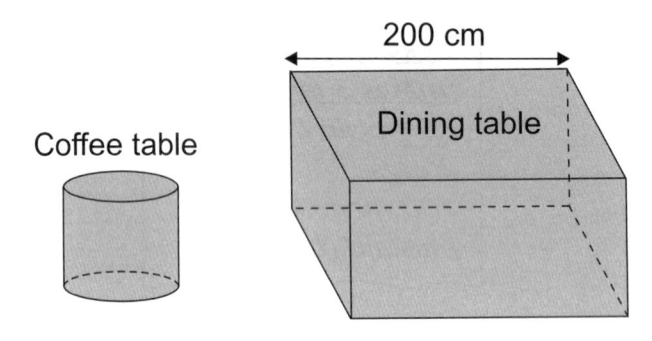

200 cm

Coffee table   Dining table

(i) Is the table cloth long enough to cover Arthur's dining table?

....

....

....
(2 marks)

(ii) What shape is Arthur's coffee table?

....
(1 mark)

(d) Arthur has champagne for after dinner.

0.75 L   125 ml

How many glasses can Arthur pour from one bottle?

....

....

....
(2 marks)

Test-style Questions

Task 3 — Buying a Car

3. You are looking for a new car.
You want to find a car that can seat 4 people, has 5 doors, is under £12 000 and has driven less than 20 000 miles.

Brand of Car	Number of seats	Number of doors
Towlio 500	5	5
Theo	5	3
Braz-racer	2	3
The Min-ute	5	5
The Fell Ranger	5	5

Car for sale - Fell Ranger
£15 450
In great condition.
19 743 miles on the clock.
Call Twinsbury 715703

Car for sale - Min-ute
£7 450
Good value.
32 490 miles driven.
Great family car.
Call Brindford 580497

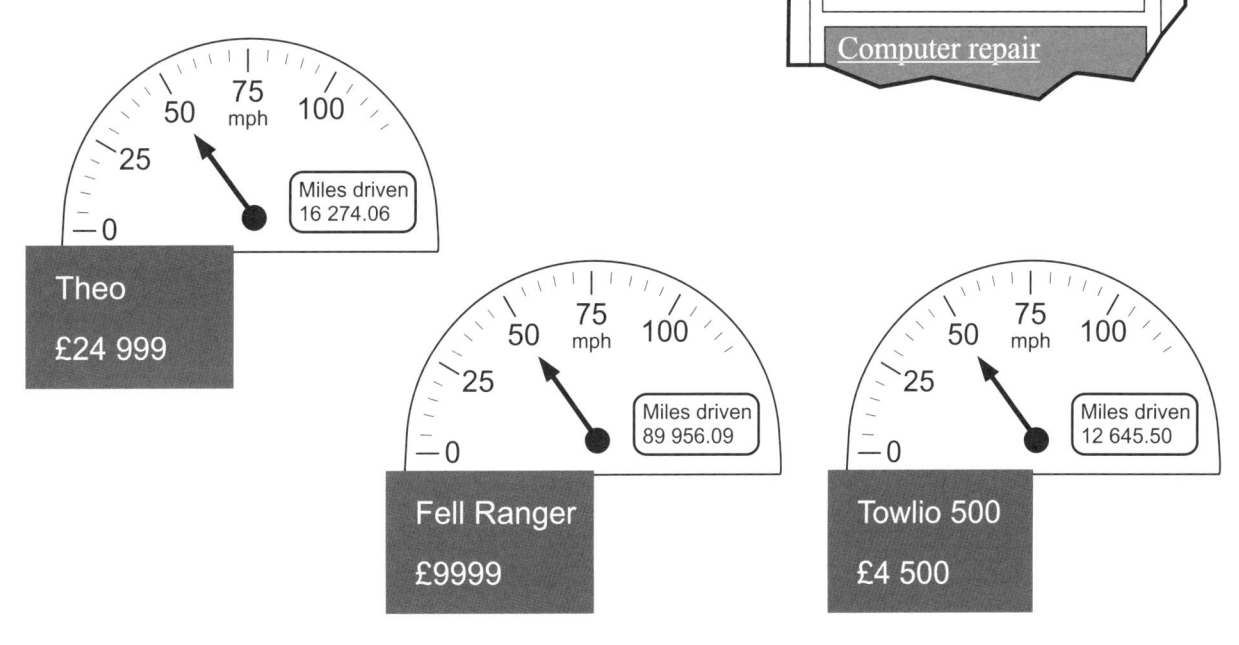

Computer repair

Theo — £24 999 — Miles driven 16 274.06

Fell Ranger — £9999 — Miles driven 89 956.09

Towlio 500 — £4 500 — Miles driven 12 645.50

(a) Which car should you buy?
List your car's features and explain why you chose it.

....

....

....

....

....

(3 marks)

Table 1 shows the insurance groups of some cars.
Table 2 shows the costs of insuring cars in the different insurance groups.

Brand of Car	Insurance Group
Towlio 500	9
Theo	50
Braz-racer	50
The Min-ute	9
The Fell Ranger	33

Table 1

Insurance group	One-off yearly fee	Cost per month for minimum 12 months
1-10	£300	£30
11-20	£400	£35
21-30	£600	£55
31-40	£1000	£87
41-50	£1500	£130

Table 2

(b) (i) How much does it cost to insure your chosen car for one year if you pay monthly?

....

....

....
(3 marks)

(ii) Should you pay a one-off fee for the year or pay monthly?
Give a reason for your answer.

....

....

....
(2 marks)

The plan below shows your drive and garage.

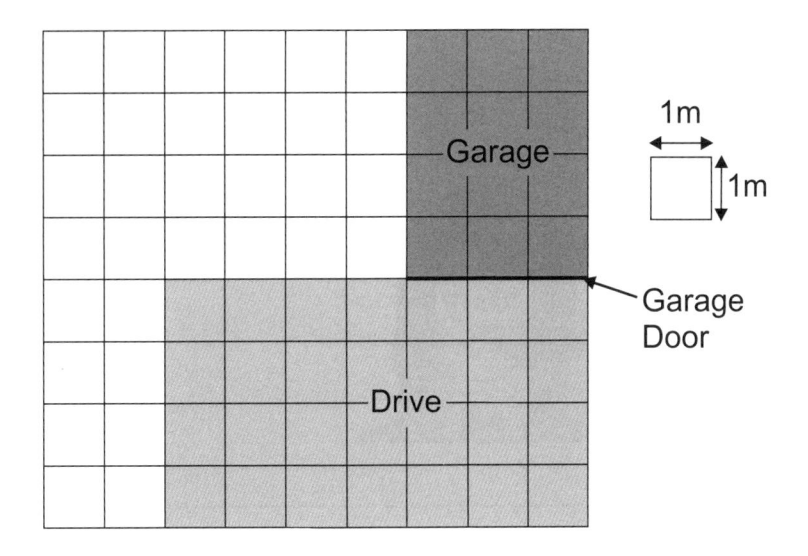

(c) (i) What shape is your garage?

....
(1 mark)

(ii) Your new car is 1.9 m wide. Does it fit into your garage?
Explain your answer.

....

....

....
(2 marks)

(d) What is the perimeter of your drive?

....

....

....
(2 marks)

Task 4 — Going on Holiday

4. Lola is planning a snowboarding trip to Val d'Essert.
Lola says:

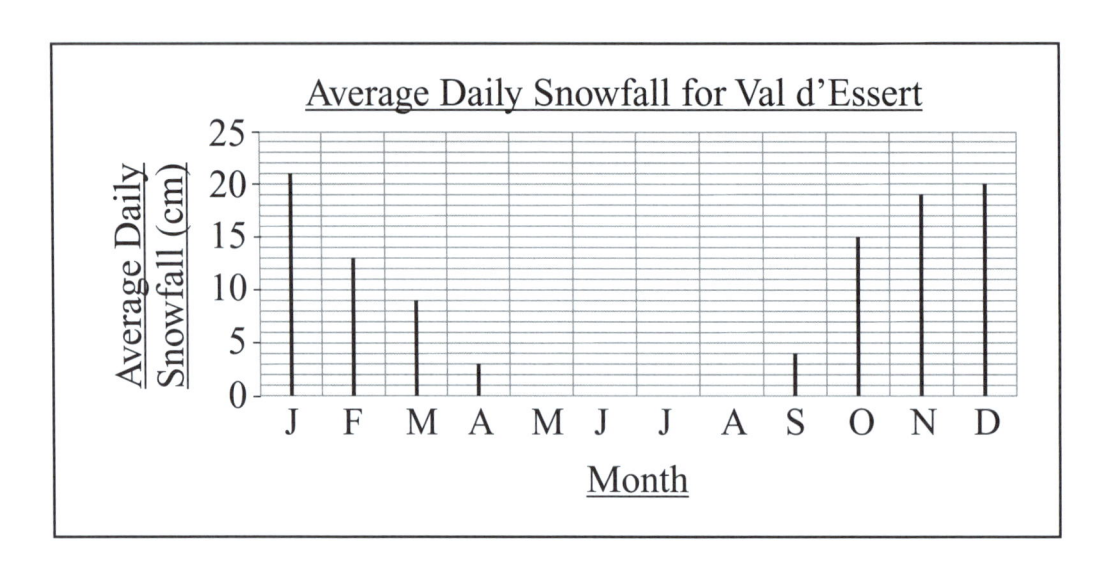

November has the highest snowfall.

Average Daily Snowfall for Val d'Essert

(a) Is Lola right?
Give a reason for your answer.

....

....
(2 marks)

(b) Lola can get a discount if she goes in October.
What is the average daily snowfall in October rounded to the nearest 10?

....

....
(2 marks)

Test-style Questions

5. There are flights to Val d'Essert on Fridays and Mondays at 16:00.
Lola wants to go for 3 nights.

Mon 2	Tues 3 Dave's bday - meal out	Wed 4	Thurs 5	Fri 6	Sat 7	Sun 8 Jill's Wedding
Mon 9 Dr's 9 am	Tues 10	Wed 11	Thurs 12	Fri 13	Sat 14	Sun 15
Mon 16	Tues 17 Football 7.30pm	Wed 18	Thurs 19	Fri 20	Sat 21 Spa day	Sun 22

(a) Choose which day Lola should fly out. Give a reason for your choice.

....

....

....
(2 marks)

(b) (i) The flight is 4 ½ hours long. At what time would Lola land?

....

....
(1 mark)

(ii) It will take Lola half an hour to travel from the airport to her hotel. Once she gets to the hotel she will have dinner. Then she will meet some friends for drinks.

Draw a possible timetable for Lola's evening in the space below.

(3 marks)
Test-style Questions

6. Lola has saved £600 for her trip.
She has made a list of all the things she needs to pay for.

Snowboarding Costs:

Return Flights:	£245.00
Hotel:	£164.00
Insurance:	£52.50
Train to and from airport:	£43.50

(a) How much money does Lola need in total?

....

....
(1 mark)

(b) How much money will Lola have left over for spending money?

....
(1 mark)

(c) How much will Lola have left over for spending money if her dad gives her a lift to and from the airport?

....

....

....
(2 marks)

Test-style Questions

7. Lola can only take liquids onto the plane in containers with a capacity of 100 ml or less.

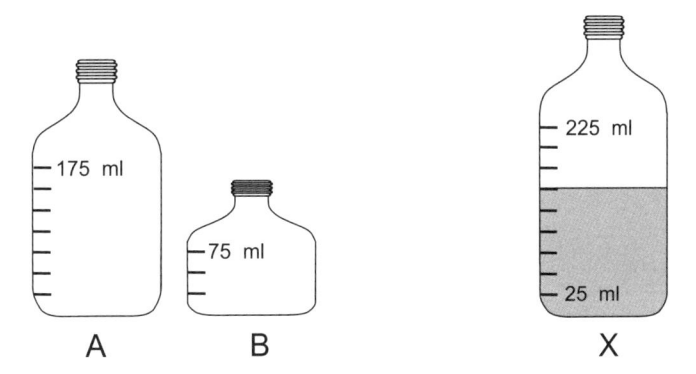

(a) Should Lola take container A or container B on the plane?

....
(1 mark)

(b) (i) How much hand cream will she have left if she takes 100 ml from container X?

....
(2 marks)

(ii) Check your calculation.

....
(1 mark)

8. Lola is buying some crisps on the plane.

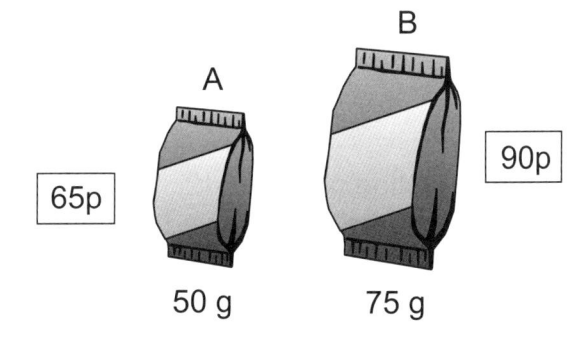

Which bag is the best value for money? Give a reason for your answer.

....

....

....
(3 marks)

Test-style Questions

Task 5 — A Car Boot Sale

9. Frank is going to sell some things at a car boot sale.
    The sale is on Wednesday the 23rd.

    (a) Mark the date on the calendar below with a tick (✓).

    (1 mark)

Mon	Tues	Wed	Thurs	Fri	Sat	Sun
	1	2	3	4	5	6
7	8	9	10	Cinema 11	12	13
14	Netball? 15	16	17	18	19	20
21	22	23	24	Christmas!! (25)	At mum's 26	27
28	29	30	31			

    (b) Frank decides to sell his stamp collection.

    (i) He has 878 UK stamps and 436 foreign stamps.
    How many of each type of stamp does he have to the nearest 100?

    ....

    ....
    (2 marks)

    (ii) Frank sets the stamp collection price at £42.
    No one is interested, so he decides to halve the price each hour until it sells.
    The car boot sale starts at 8:00 and Frank sells the stamp collection at 10:00.
    How much did Frank sell the stamp collection for?

    ....

    ....

    ....
    (3 marks)

(c) Frank also decides to sell his beer mat collection.
One customer is only interested in circular beer mats.

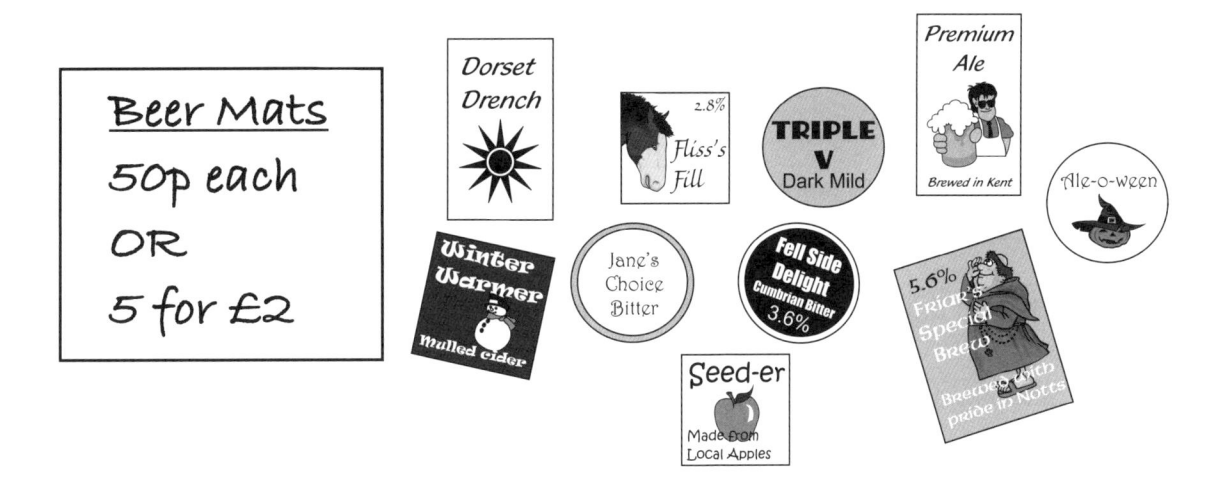

(i) How many circular beer mats does Frank have?

....
(1 mark)

(ii) Should the customer buy the beer mats separately or as part of the deal?
Give a reason for your answer.

....

....

....
(2 marks)

(d) Frank makes a table to show how much money he made on some of the different items he has sold.

	Money
Beer mats	£5.75
CDs	£36.49
Thimbles	£5.53
Books	£11.98

i) Which item did he make the most money on?

....
(1 mark)

ii) Estimate how much money Frank made in total.

....

....

....
(2 marks)

Answers — Practice Questions

Section One — Number

Page 4
Q1 3
Q2 210
Q3 Dorothy
Q4 a) Jane
    b) Sarah
Q5 a) Large silver
    b) Small silver

Page 8
Q1 5
Q2 39
Q3 16
Q4 78
Q5 £17
Q6 405
Q7 17p
Q8 120
Q9 86
    86 − 49 = 37 OR
    86 − 37 = 49

Page 11
Q1 140
Q2 12
Q3 125
Q4 Yes (he has 70 screws)
Q5 a) 250 sheets
    b) 750 sheets
Q6 6 packs
Q7 12 bunches

Page 12
Q1 60
    60 ÷ 6 = 10 OR
    60 ÷ 10 = 6
Q2 25 jars
    25 × 5 = 125
Q3 2 packs
    12 × 1 = 12 (not enough)
    12 × 2 = 24 (enough)

Page 15
Q1 Smaller
Q2 £6.43
Q3 Yes
Q4 No
Q5 3.4, 6.2, 7.8, 7.9
Q6 Jess
Q7 Oliver

Page 17
Q1 4.98
Q2 5.49
Q3 17.5
Q4 0.78
Q5 £23.85
Q6 £12.49
Q7 No (he has only spent £4.40)
Q8 132 miles
Q9 5.25 g
Q10 £12.25

Page 18
Q1 $\frac{1}{2}$
Q2 a) 1
    b) $\frac{1}{4}$

Page 21
Q1 0.75
Q2 3
Q3 110
Q4 £187.50
Q5 £280
Q6 a) 7
    b) 21

Page 23
Q1 a) 130
    b) 100
Q2 600
Q3 £6

Page 25
Q1 E.g. 600 + 100 = 700
    OR 620 + 80 = 700.
Q2 100 + 50 + 20 = 170
Q3 £40 × 20 = £800
Q4 £20 − £2 − £3 − £1 − £1 − £4
    = £9
Q5 6 m

Page 27
Q1 10, 14, 18, 22, 26, 30
Q2 240

Section Two — Measure

Page 30
Q1 metre
Q2 gram
Q3 millilitre
Q4 a) <u>metres</u> and <u>centimetres</u>
    b) <u>g</u> and <u>kg</u>
    c) <u>litres</u>
Q5 1000 (m)
Q6 1000 (g)
Q7 100 (cl)
Q8 a) centimetre
    b) kilometre
    c) centilitre

Page 31
Q1 6 km
Q2 35 m
Q3 5.5 m

Page 32
Q1 200 cm (or 2 m)
Q2 28 beads

Page 33
Q1 Tony can choose from rugs 1, 3 and 5.

Page 34
Q1 E.g. each car needs about 2 m of space. So the row of spaces will be 16 m long.
    You could have a different answer here as long as it's sensible.

Page 36
Q1 18 cm
Q2 7.25 m

Page 38
Q1 72.5 kg
Q2 4
Q3 650 g

Page 39
Q1 Sleeper Light
Q2 Tuna Mayonnaise
Q3 E.g. 55 kg + 60 kg = 115 kg

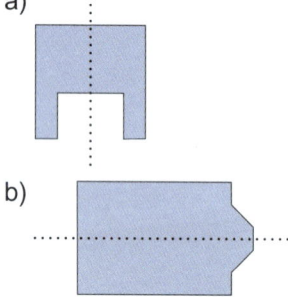

Page 41
Q1 a) 500 ml
   b) 200 ml
Q2 7.5 L
Q3 7.2 L
Q4 200 ml (or 0.2 L)

Page 43
Q1 Herald 175 or AEB 224
Q2 85 ml
Q3 A: 500 ml
   B: 250 ml
   A is about half full and B is about a quarter full.

Page 45
Q1 38 °C
Q2 0 °C
Q3 a) 1.5 °C
   b) Monday
Q4 190 °C

Page 46
Q1 a) E.g. 9 °C (accept 8-12 °C)
   In March, it's likely to be warmer than in January, but cooler than in May.
   b) E.g. 22 °C (accept 16-23 °C)
   In July, it's likely to be warmer than in May but it must be cooler than 24 °C.

Page 48
Q1 3.5 cm (or 35 mm)
Q2 a) 300 ml
   b) 150 ml
   c) 50 ml

Page 49
Q1 2 °C
Q2 170 kg

Page 51
Q1 a) 384p
   b) 127p
Q2 a) £0.61
   b) £2.31
Q3 A pen costing £0.69.
Q4 £1.48
Q5 £3.55

Page 52
Q1 £22.50
Q2 No (she wants to spend £65).

Page 53
Q1 8 bread rolls for £2.40.
Q2 The 450 g tin for 72p.

Section Three — Dates and Time

Page 55
Q1 a) the 13th of May
   b) the 19th of May
   c) the 18th of May

Page 56
Q1 30 minutes
Q2 365 days
Q3 21 days

Page 57
Q1 a) 10:30 am
   b) 3:35 pm
Q2 a) 19:10
   b) 05:20
Q3 Yes, he is late (by 30 minutes).

Page 59
Q1 2 and a half hours (or 2.5 hours or 150 minutes).
Q2 55 minutes
Q3 4 hours and 15 minutes (or 4.25 hours or 255 minutes)
Q4 19:30 (or 7:30 pm)
Q5 6:40 pm (or 18:40)
Q6 1 hour and 45 minutes (or 1.75 hours or 105 minutes)

Page 62
Q1 a) The 16:55 train.
   b) Yes, she can still catch the same train (it arrives before 17:15).
Q2 a) 13:30
   b) 1 hour and 45 minutes (or an hour and three quarters).
   c) Afternoon break.
Q3 For example:

Activity	Start	Finish
Guests arriving	7.30 pm	8.00 pm
Catwalk	8.00 pm	9.00 pm
Party	9.00 pm	11.00 pm

There are lots of different ways you can do this timetable. Just make sure you've included all the information in the question.

Section Four — Shape and Space

Page 63
Q1 B
Q2 a) 0
   b) 4
   c) 1

Page 65
Q1 a)
   b)
Q2 a) 2
   b) 1
   c) 0
   d) 2

Page 68
Q1 a) circle
   b) square
   c) rectangle
   d) triangle
   e) rectangle
   f) triangle
Q2 B
Q3 rectangle

Page 70
Q1 a) cylinder
   b) cube
   c) cuboid
Q2 cuboid
Q3 A
Q4 A cylinder (top) and a cube (bottom).

Answers — Practice Questions

Page 72
Q1 a) A circle
    b) Any square that's 4 squares big, placed in a sensible place. For example:

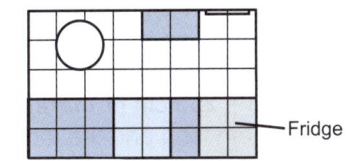

Q2 Any square that's 4 squares big, placed next to the bed. For example:

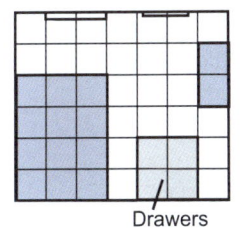

Page 74
Q1 a) east
    b) clockwise
    c) south

Section Five — Handling Data

Page 76
Q1 a) 0.9 kg
    b) Thom
Q2 a) £2.80
    b) £0.10 / 10p

Page 79
Q1 a) 07:03
    b) 19:01
    c) Wednesday
Q2 a) 40
    b) 175
    c) 123
Q3 lamp shade

Page 80
Q1 a) 4
    b) 10
    c)

Favourite type of holiday	Tally
Beach	IIII
Skiing	ЖI
Safari	Ж II
Cruise	Ж Ж
Sightseeing	Ж I

Page 82
Q1 a) 6
    b) 5
    c) Thursday
Q2 a) 0
    b) by bus
    c) by car
    d) 1

Page 83
Q1 a) 4 °C
    b) 7 °C

Answers — Test-style Questions

Task 1 — An Evening Out (Page 85)

1. a) i) 7.30 pm + 12 hours = 19:30 **(1 mark)**
      ii) 1835 **(1 mark)**
   They could catch an earlier bus, but then they'd be very early to the play.
   b) i) Student tickets in the circle cost £25 each.
         So £25 + £25 = £50 **(1 mark)**.
      ii) Student tickets in the stalls cost £28 each.
         So £28 + £28 = £56 **(1 mark)**.
         To find out how much more expensive it is to sit in the stalls, take the circle price away from the stalls price. £56 − £50 = £6 more expensive **(1 mark)**.
   If you didn't get £50 for b)i) you'll have got a different answer to b)ii). You can still get the mark, as long as you use your answer to b)i) and the right method.
   c) i) One double-scoop ice cream costs £2.50.
         So £2.50 + £2.50 = £5.00 **(1 mark)**.
      ii) They only pay half with the offer, so £5.00 × 1 ÷ 2 = £2.50 **(1 mark)**.
   If you didn't get £5.00 for c)i) you'll have got a different answer to c)ii). You can still get the marks, as long as you use your answer to c)i) and the right method.
   d) i) 10 miles × £1.25 = £12.50 **(1 mark)**.
      ii) £12.50 ÷ 10 = £1.25 OR
         £12.50 ÷ £1.25 = 10 **(1 mark)**.

Task 2 — Hosting a Dinner Party (Page 88)

2. a) i) First work out how many Tasty Treats Arthur needs in total: 6 people × 3 Tasty Treats each = 6 × 3 = 18
         (1 mark for 6 × 3, 1 mark for 18).
         Now out how many boxes Arthur needs to buy. There are 5 Treats per box, so: 18 ÷ 5 = 3.6
         (1 mark for 18 ÷ 5, 1 mark for 3.6).
         3.6 isn't a whole number, so Arthur will need to buy 4 packs **(1 mark)**.
      ii) 7.15 pm + 0.30 = 7.45 pm is when the Tasty Treats should be served **(1 mark)**. They take 15 mins to cook, so 7.45 pm − 0.15 = 7.30. The Tasty Treats should be put in the oven at 7.30 pm **(1 mark)**.
   b) i) 3 × 2 = 6, so to make 6 Yorkshire puddings, Arthur needs 2 times as much flour.
         So 70 g × 2 = 140 g **(1 mark for correct calculation, 1 mark for the correct answer)**.
      ii) 50 g on the scales already **(1 mark)**.
         So he needs to weigh out 140 g − 50 g = 90 g more flour **(1 mark)**.
         Check: 90 g + 50 g = 140 g **(1 mark)**.
   If you read the scales wrong, you will get a different answer to the ones given above. But you can still get some marks if your subtraction calculation and check calculation are correct.

   c) i) The length of the table cloth is given in m and the length of the table is given in cm. So you need to convert the length of the table cloth into cm. 2.55 m × 100 = 255 cm **(1 mark)**. The table cloth is 255 cm long and the table is 200 cm long. So yes, the table cloth will cover the table **(1 mark)**.
      ii) It's a cylinder **(1 mark)**.
   d) The volume of the bottle is given in L and the volume of the glass is given in ml. So you need to convert the volume of the bottle into ml.
      0.75 L × 1000 = 750 ml **(1 mark)**.
      750 ml ÷ 125 ml = 6 glasses **(1 mark)**.

Task 3 — Buying a Car (Page 91)

3. a) Towlio 500. It has driven 12 645.50 miles, it costs £4 500, it can seat 5 people and has 5 doors. I chose it because it has driven less than 20 000 miles, costs less than £12 000, can seat 4 people and has 5 doors **(1 mark listing your chosen car's features, 1 mark for some evidence that you've considered at least 3 of the requirements in the question, 1 mark for Towlio 500)**.
   b) i) The Towlio 500 is in insurance group 9 **(1 mark)**. Groups 1-10 cost £30 per month to insure **(1 mark)**. So the total cost of insurance for the year = £30 × 12 = £360 **(1 mark)**.
      ii) One-off **(1 mark)**.
         Because it is £60 cheaper to pay it this way: £360 − £300 = £60 **(1 mark)**.
   If you didn't get the Towlio 500 for a) you'll have got different answers to b)i) and ii). You can still get the marks, as long as you use your answers all the way through.
   c) i) A rectangle **(1 mark)**.
      ii) Each square has sides that are 1 m wide. The garage door is three squares long, and so is 3 m wide **(1 mark)**. This is bigger than the car (1.9 m), so yes the car fits in the garage **(1 mark)**.
   d) 7 squares on the top = 7 m. 4 squares on the right side = 4 m. 7 squares on the bottom = 7 m. 4 squares on the left side = 4 m.
      7 + 4 + 7 + 4 = 22 m **(1 mark for correct calculation, 1 mark for correct answer)**.

Task 4 — Going on Holiday (Page 94)

4 a) No *(1 mark)*. January and December get more snow *(1 mark)*.
   b) 15 cm is the average daily snowfall in October *(1 mark)*. This rounds up to 20 cm *(1 mark)*.
5 a) Mon 9 OR Fri 13 *(1 mark)*. These are the only days when flights leave and Lola has nothing on for three nights following that flight *(1 mark)*.

The Monday flight is at 4 pm, so Lola should still make this even with the Dr's appointment in the morning.

   b) i) 16:00 + 4½ hours = 20:30 or 8.30 pm *(1 mark)*.
      ii) For example:

Activity:	Time:
Land at airport	20.30
Arrive at hotel	21.00
Dinner	21.15
Drinks	22.00

   (1 mark for arriving at the hotel at least half an hour after landing, 1 mark for including dinner after arriving at the hotel, 1 mark for including drinks after dinner.)

There are lots of possible ways you could have drawn your timetable — this is just one example. You're not told how long dinner should last in the question, so you need to decide this yourself.

6 a) Add up all the costs.
      £245 + £164 + £52.50 + £43.50 = £505 *(1 mark)*.
   b) £600 − £505 = £95 *(1 mark)*.
   c) Add up the costs except the train tickets.
      £245 + £164 + £52.50 = £461.50
      Money left over: £600 − £461.50 = £138.50
      OR
      Add the cost of the train tickets to the amount of spending money she already has:
      £95 + £43.50 = £138.50. **(1 mark for any correct calculation, 1 mark for the correct answer)**
7 a) B *(1 mark)*.
   b) i) 150 ml − 100 ml = 50 ml
          (1 mark for correctly reading off 150 ml, 1 mark for correct answer).
      ii) 100 ml + 50 ml = 150 ml *(1 mark)*.

Your answer to this might be different if you didn't read the correct volume off the diagram for question b)i). But as long as your check shows the correct check for your calculation to b)i) you'll still get the mark.

8 65p ÷ 50 g = 1.3p per g *(1 mark)*.
   90p ÷ 75 g = 1.2p per g *(1 mark)*.
   Bag B is better value as it costs less per gram *(1 mark)*.

Task 5 — A Car Boot Sale (Page 98)

9 a) *(1 mark for a tick in the correct place as shown below)*.

Mon	Tues	Wed	Thurs	Fri	Sat	Sun
	1	2	3	4	5	6
7	8	9	10	Cinema 11	12	13
14	Netball? 15	16	17	18	19	20
21	22	✓ 23	24	Christmas!! 25	At mum's 26	27
28	29	30	31			

   b) i) 900 UK stamps *(1 mark)*.
          400 foreign stamps *(1 mark)*.
      ii) The price halves every hour, so it should be divided by 2 every hour.
          10:00 − 8:00 = 2 hours *(1 mark)*.
          £42 ÷ 2 = £21 *(1 mark)*.
          £21 ÷ 2 = £10.50. Arthur sold the stamp collection for £10.50 *(1 mark)*.
   c) i) 4 *(1 mark)*.
      ii) 4 × 50p = 200p / £2.00 *(1 mark)*.
          For second mark:
          The customer should go for the deal as they pay the same price, but they get one more beer mat *(1 mark)*.
          OR
          The customer should pay for them separately as it's the same price and they only want circular ones *(1 mark)*.

It doesn't matter if you go for the deal or not, it's the calculation and the reason for your answer that is important.

   d) i) CDs *(1 mark)*.
      ii) E.g.
          Money made on beer mats = £5.75
          Money made on CDs = about £36.50
          Money made on thimbles = about £5.50
          Money made on books = about £12.00.
          Total money made =
          £5.75 + £36.50 + £5.50 + £12.00 = £59.75
          (1 mark for sensible rounding estimates for at least 3 items, 1 mark for correctly adding together these estimates)

You might get a different answer to this question, depending on how much you rounded by. As long as your rounding and final calculation is correct, you should still get the marks.

Answers — Test-style Questions

Glossary

12-hour clock

The 12 hour clock goes from 12:00 am (midnight) to 11:59 am (one minute before noon), and then from 12:00 pm (noon) till 11:59 pm (one minute before midnight).

24-hour clock

The 24 hour clock goes from 00:00 (midnight) to 23:59 (one minute before the next midnight).

2D shape

A flat shape.

3D shape

A solid shape.

A

Angle

A measurement that tells you the size of a corner.

Anticlockwise

Movement in the opposite direction to the hands of a clock.

B

Bar Chart

A chart which shows information using bars.

C

Capacity

How much something will hold. For example, a beaker with a capacity of 200 ml can hold 200 ml of liquid.

Circle

A 2D shape with one curved side and no corners.

Clockwise

Movement in the same direction as the hands of a clock.

Compass Points

The four directions in which a compass points. These are: North, South, East and West.

Cube

A 3D shape in which all the flat parts are squares.

Cuboid

A 3D shape in which some of the flat parts are rectangles.

Cylinder

A 3D shape in which two of the flat parts are circles. A cylinder has no corners.

D

Data

Another word for information.

Decimal Number

A number with a decimal point (.) in it. For example, 0.75.

Digit

One of these: 0 1 2 3 4 5 6 7 8 9. All numbers are made by putting these digits together. For example: 22, 359.

E

Estimate

A close guess at what an answer will be.

F

Fraction

A way of showing parts of a whole. For example: ¼ (one quarter).

L

Length

How long something is. Length can be measured in different units, for example, millimetres (mm), centimetres (cm), or metres (m).

Line Graph
A graph which shows data using a line.

Line of Symmetry
A shape with a line of symmetry has two halves that are mirror images of each other. If the shape is folded along this line, the two sides will fold exactly together.

List
A simple way of showing information. For example, a shopping list shows what you need to buy from the shops.

N

Number Pattern
A list of numbers that follow a pattern.

P

Perimeter
The distance around the outside of a shape.

Plan
A diagram to show the layout of an area. For example, the layout of objects in a room.

R

Rectangle
A 2D shape with 4 sides. Sides that are opposite each other are the same length. The angles at the corners are all right angles.

Right angle
Square corners.

S

Scale
Something you use to measure things. For example, you can use the scale on a ruler to measure length.

Square
A 2D shape with 4 sides. All the sides are the same length. The angles at the corners are all right angles.

Symmetry
See line of symmetry.

T

Table
A way of showing data. In a table, data is arranged into columns and rows.

Tally Chart
A chart used for putting data into different categories. You use tally marks (lines) to record each piece of data in the chart.

Temperature
A number that shows how hot or cold something is. Degrees Celsius (°C) are common units for temperature.

Timetable
A table with information about when things will happen.

Triangle
A 2D shape with 3 straight sides and 3 corners.

U

Unit
A way of showing what type of number you've got. For example, metres (m) or grams (g).

V

Volume
The amount of space something takes up.

W

Weight
How heavy something is. Grams (g) and kilograms (kg) are common units for weight.

Glossary

Index

2D shapes 66-68
3D shapes 69
12-hour clock 57
24-hour clock 57

A
adding 5-7
angles 63
anticlockwise 73

B
bar charts 81

C
calculators 7
calendars 54, 55
capacity 29, 40-42
circles 68
clockwise 73
compass points 74
cubes 69
cuboids 69
cylinders 69

D
data 75
decimals 13-16
digits 1
directions 73, 74
dividing 9, 10, 12

E
estimating 24, 25

F
fractions 18-21

L
length 28, 31-34, 47
line graphs 83
lines of symmetry 64, 65
lists 75, 76

M
money 50-53
multiplying 9, 10, 12

N
number lines 13
number patterns 26, 27

P
pence 50
perimeter 35
plans 71, 72
pounds 50
price per gram 53
price per item 53

R
rectangles 67
right angles 63
rounding 22, 23

S
scales (reading) 47-49
subtracting 6, 7
symmetry 64, 65

T
tables 77, 78
tally charts 80
temperature 44-46, 49
thermometer 49
time 56-58
timetables 60, 61

U
units 28, 29, 50, 56
   of capacity 29
   of length 28
   of money 50
   of time 56
   of weight 29

V
value for money 53
volume 40-42, 47

W
weight 29, 37, 38, 48